Developing Listening Skills 1

Second Edition

Casey Malarcher

Compass Publishing

Developing Listening Skills 1 Second Edition

Casey Malarcher

Acquisitions Editor: John Thomas
Illustrator: Hieram Weintraub
Design: Design Plus

email: info@compasspub.com
http://www.compasspub.com

ISBN: 978-1-59966-526-9

10 9 8 7 6 5 4
13 12 11

Photo Credits

All images © Shutterstock, Inc. except: p. 8 © iStock International Inc.

CONTENTS

36 Topics of *Developing Listening Skills, Second Edition*

UNIT	BOOK 1	BOOK 2	BOOK 3
UNIT 1	First Meeting	Entertainment	Locations
UNIT 2	Family and Friends	Shopping	Promises
UNIT 3	Free Time	Work	Special Occasions
UNIT 4	Date and Time	Computers	Steps and Plans
UNIT 5	Telephone	Travel	Music
UNIT 6	Directions	Restaurants	Groups
UNIT 7	Schools	Hotels	Outdoors
UNIT 8	Sports	Transportation	Meetings
UNIT 9	Appearance	Banks	Feelings
UNIT 10	Weather	Driving	Favors
UNIT 11	Instructions	Housing	Memories
UNIT 12	Stories	Health	Assistance

First Meeting

Warm-up

Listen to the dialogs. (((Track 1)))

Listen again, and fill in the blanks. (((Track 2)))

1. Joe knows Karen's _____.
2. Larry didn't _____ Gloria.
3. Greg introduces his _____ to Sarah.
4. Ellen and Steve both know _____.

Write the missing words to make correct expressions.

believe	catch	do	going	met
mind	nice	pleasure	see	up

1. Do you _____ if I sit here?
2. Have we _____ before?
3. I didn't _____ your name.
4. How do you _____?
5. It's _____ to meet you.

6. Long time no _____.
7. How is it _____?
8. I don't _____ we've met.
9. What's _____?
10. It's a _____ to meet you.

Listening Practice

A

How would you answer?

Listen. Write the answer. ((Track 3))

Hi, I'm Paula.	Not at all. Have a seat.	Not much.
I'm fine, thank you.	No, I don't believe we have.	

1. _____
2. _____
3. _____
4. _____
5. _____

B

How would you ask?

Listen. Write the question or statement. ((Track 4))

How is it going?	It's a pleasure to meet you.	What's up?
Is this seat taken?	Hi, I'm Lisa. What's your name?	

1. _____
2. _____
3. _____
4. _____
5. _____

C

Picture Description

Describe the picture using the words below.

trees	stand	talk	book

✓ **Listen to the description of the picture.** ((Track 5))

Speaking Practice

A
Intonation Practice

In speech, content words (nouns, verbs, adjectives, and adverbs) are stressed, while function words (articles, auxiliary verbs, prepositions, conjunctions, and pronouns) are not usually stressed. In the following statements and questions, study the stressed words that are in bold letters.

Written	Spoken
1. My name is Ellen.	1. My **name** is **Ellen**.
2. I don't believe we've met.	2. I don't **believe** we've **met**.
3. Where do you know Alex from?	3. **Where** do you **know Alex** from?

✓ **Now practice saying the following sentences. Remember to stress the content words, but not the function words.**

1. Nice to meet you, too.
2. Do you come here to ski often?
3. I'll be your guide for today's tour.

✓ **Now listen and repeat.** ((Track 6))

B
Conversation Pictures

Listen to the dialogs, and number the pictures. ((Track 7))

✓ **Now listen to the dialogs again, and choose the correct relationship.**

1. (A) Classmates (B) Co-workers (C) Old friends (D) Relatives
2. (A) Classmates (B) Co-workers (C) Old friends (D) Relatives
3. (A) Classmates (B) Co-workers (C) Old friends (D) Relatives
4. (A) Classmates (B) Co-workers (C) Old friends (D) Relatives

Short Dialogs

Dialog 1

Listen to the dialog and questions. Choose the best answer. ((Track 8))

1. (A) At a party   (B) In a classroom
   (C) On a bus   (D) On the street

2. (A) Their address   (B) Their ages
   (C) Their names   (D) Their friends

✓ **Listen again, and fill in the blanks.**

W: Excuse me, is this seat taken?

M: No, it's not. Please ❶_____.

W: Thanks. My name is Julia.

M: Hi, Julia. I'm Rick. Nice ❷_____ you.

W: Nice to meet you, too. Wow! There sure are a lot of students in this ❸_____.

M: Yeah. This class is required for all ❹_____.

B

Dialog 2

Listen to the dialog and questions. Choose the best answer. ((Track 9))

1. (A) To ask her questions   (B) To find out her name
   (C) To make friends   (D) To welcome her

2. (A) Ask him questions   (B) Leave the office
   (C) Talk to freshmen   (D) Talk to him

C

Dialog 3

Listen to the dialog, and complete each statement. ((Track 10))

1. Tanya heard about Doug from

   _____.

2. Doug tells Tanya that he doesn't know

   _____.

Main Dialog

A

Listen

Listen to the dialog, and choose the best answer. ((Track 11))

1. Which is true about the woman and the man?
   - (A) They are in the wrong seats.
   - (B) They are friends traveling together.
   - (C) They don't know each other.
   - (D) They work for the same airline.

2. Who talks about his or her job?
   - (A) The woman
   - (B) The man
   - (C) Both of them
   - (D) Neither of them

3. What do we learn about the man?
   - (A) His age
   - (B) His home town
   - (C) His name
   - (D) His sister's job

B

Listen Again

Listen again, and fill in the blanks. ((Track 12))

W: Excuse me. That's my seat by the window.

M: Sorry, I'll move my jacket.

W: Thanks. This flight is really full.

M: It's the peak travel ❶_____. Are you going to Berlin for business or pleasure?

W: Business. I'm ❷_____ at a conference there.

M: Really? What kind of conference?

W: It is a ❸_____ conference. What will you be doing in Berlin?

M: I'm visiting my ❹_____. Have you been to Germany before?

W: I've been to Europe ❺_____ times, but this is my first time visiting Germany.

M: Oh. ❻_____, I'm Phillip.

W: Nice to ❼_____ you, Phillip. I'm Wendy.

M: I've never met a ❽_____ before . . . .

Short Talks

Listen to the short talk and questions. Choose the best answer. ((Track 13))

1. (A) They work together.   (B) They have similar interests.
   (C) They like to go to parties.   (D) They fell in love.

2. (A) At a conference   (B) At a party
   (C) In a store   (D) On an airplane

✓ **Listen again, and fill in the blanks.**

I met this really interesting woman named Olivia
❶_____ last weekend. She said she
works for a ❷_____ company. As we were
talking, I found out she used to work as a professional
❸_____. This surprised me because I like
❹_____, too. It's my hobby.

Listen to the short talk and questions. Choose the best answer. ((Track 14))

1. (A) A book   (B) A class
   (C) A club   (D) A conference

2. (A) Call   (B) Go online
   (C) Mail in a form   (D) Meet on Oct. 3rd

Listen to the short talk. Match the information that goes together. ((Track 15))

1. The speaker thought that •   • (A) he really didn't know her.

2. The girl laughed because •   • (B) he saw a girl named Pam.

3. Then he found out that •   • (C) she is a neighbor of his brother's
                                            friend.

Listening Quiz

A

Picture Matching

Listen to the dialogs. Choose the correct picture. ((Track 16))

 **A**  **B**  **C**

1. (A)　　　(B)　　　(C)

2. (A)　　　(B)　　　(C)

B

Listen & Choose

Listen to the dialogs and questions. Choose the best answer. ((Track 17))

3. (A) They don't know each other.　(B) They know each other.
　 (C) They study together.　　　　(D) They work together.

4. (A) In a dormitory　　　　(B) In a park
　 (C) In a store　　　　　　(D) On an airplane

5. (A) Their ages　　　　　(B) Their hometowns
　 (C) Their jobs　　　　　(D) Their names

6. (A) The woman's friend　　(B) The woman's neighbor
　 (C) The woman's aunt　　　(D) The woman's colleague

7. (A) The food　　　　(B) The people
　 (C) The weekend　　(D) The weather

8. (A) Mary　　　　　　(B) Dottie
　 (C) Ms. Williams　　(D) Mrs. Williams

9. (A) In a classroom　　(B) In a house
　 (C) In an office　　　(D) At a bus stop

Wrap-up

A

Pre-listening Discussion

Talk about these questions.

1. What do you talk about when you meet someone for the first time?
2. What shouldn't you talk about when you meet someone for the first time?
3. What are "taboo" topics you shouldn't talk about when you meet Americans?

B

Listening Comprehension

Listen and answer the questions. ((Track 18))

1. **Who asks the speaker about American culture?**
   The people who ask her about American culture are _____.
2. **When does the speaker shake hands?**
   The speaker shakes hands when the other person _____.
3. **What should the speaker's friends first talk about when they meet new people?**
   The speaker suggests that they should talk about _____ or _____.

C

Dictation Practice

Listen again, and fill in the blanks. ((Track 19))

There are lots of students ❶_____ other countries at my school. ❷_____ very interesting to meet them, ❸_____ I have made ❹_____ with lots of international students. Sometimes they ❺_____ me questions about American culture. ❻_____ don't always know exactly how ❼_____ answer their questions, but I ❽_____ my best.

These friends often ask, "What ❾_____ the polite way to greet ❿_____ American?" My answer is simple: smile. ⓫_____ also shake hands during introductions, ⓬_____ not everyone does this. It's ⓭_____ for me to see what ⓮_____ other person will do first. ⓯_____ they put out their hand, ⓰_____ we'll shake, but for most ⓱_____, it's enough just to smile ⓲_____ say hello.

My friends also ask, "What ⓳_____ Americans talk about when they ⓴_____ new people?" This question is ㉑_____ to answer, but you should ㉒_____ someone well before you talk ㉓_____ certain things. I suggest that my ㉔_____ friends talk about where they ㉕_____ or what they are doing. ㉖_____ example, if they meet a ㉗_____ person at school, talk about ㉘_____. If they meet a new ㉙_____ at a party, talk about the ㉚_____. The other person might bring ㉛_____ other topics to talk about ㉜_____ that.

12 Unit 1

Listening Test 08:42 🕐

PART I: Picture Description ((Track 20))

Listen and choose the statement that best describes what you see in the picture.

1.

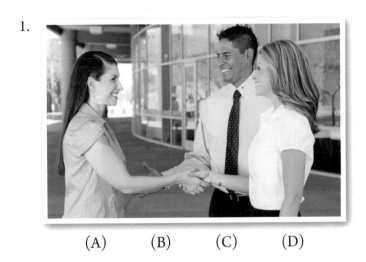

    (A)   (B)   (C)   (D)

2.

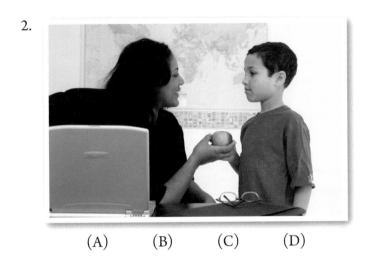

    (A)   (B)   (C)   (D)

3.

    (A)   (B)   (C)   (D)

4.

(A)   (B)   (C)   (D)

5.

(A)   (B)   (C)   (D)

PART II: Questions and Responses ((Track 21))

Listen and choose the best response to each question.

6. (A)   (B)   (C)

7. (A)   (B)   (C)

8. (A)   (B)   (C)

9. (A)   (B)   (C)

10. (A)   (B)   (C)

PART III: Short Conversations ((Track 22))

You will hear two dialogs, each followed by three questions. Listen carefully, and choose the best answer to each question.

11. Whose name is mentioned?

   (A) The man's
   (B) The woman's
   (C) The man's and the woman's
   (D) Neither the man's nor the woman's

12. What does the woman prefer to be called?

   (A) Her first name
   (B) Her full name
   (C) Her last name
   (D) Her nickname

13. Who calls the woman Ms. Little?

   (A) Children in her class
   (B) Children who live near her
   (C) Her children
   (D) Her students' children

---

14. What are the speakers doing?

   (A) Getting ready to start class
   (B) Meeting for the first time
   (C) Taking their seats on an airplane
   (D) Talking about people they both know

15. Where did the woman recently move from?

   (A) Chicago
   (B) Los Angeles
   (C) New Jersey
   (D) The man's hometown

16. What is true about Susan?

   (A) She did not like living in Chicago.
   (B) She grew up in Chicago.
   (C) She hopes to move to Chicago soon.
   (D) She now lives in Chicago.

PART IV: Short Talks ((Track 23))

You will hear two talks, each followed by three questions. Listen carefully, and choose the best answer to each question.

17. Who is introducing himself?

    (A) A freshman
    (B) A professor
    (C) A reporter
    (D) A tour guide

18. Which is true about the speaker?

    (A) He designs university buildings.
    (B) He plans to open a university.
    (C) He studies at the university.
    (D) He teaches at the university.

19. Who is the speaker probably talking to?

    (A) Parents and future students
    (B) His roommate
    (C) Students graduating from the university
    (D) University faculty

---

20. Who is the woman introducing?

    (A) A politician
    (B) A prize winner
    (C) An invited speaker
    (D) Herself

21. Which is probably true about Elizabeth Berkley?

    (A) She came from a poor family.
    (B) She has written articles and books.
    (C) She grew up on Wall Street.
    (D) She won a lot of money.

22. What will happen next?

    (A) A prize will be given to Elizabeth.
    (B) The author will begin speaking.
    (C) The audience will leave the room.
    (D) The author will read from a very old book.

UNIT 2 Family and Friends

Warm-up

A
Look & Listen

Listen to the dialogs. ((Track 24))

B
Listen Again

Listen again, and match the information with the correct person. ((Track 25))

1. Rosemary •   • (A) has a nickname.
2. Susan •   • (B) just had a baby.
3. Charles •   • (C) looks similar to one of his family members.
4. Karen •   • (D) sees the speaker once a month.

C
Essential Expressions

Write the name(s) that go with each phrase.

1. Larry's grandparents: _____ and _____
2. Amy's parents: _____ and _____
3. Emily's cousin: _____
4. Fred Jr.'s aunt: _____
5. Ellen's sister: _____
6. an only child: _____
7. an uncle who is not married: _____
8. Greg's younger brother: _____
9. Sally's oldest daughter: _____
10. a relative who passed away: _____

Family tree:
- **Don** 1918 - 1985 — **Amelia** 1922 -
  - **Fred** 1940 -
  - **Mary** 1942 -
  - **Ellen** 1945 -
  - **Kate** 1965 -
  - **Fred Jr.** 1963 -
  - **Larry** 1964 -
  - **Sally** 1967 -
  - **Charles** 1966 -
  - **Amy** 1995 -
  - **Emily** 1998 -
  - **Greg** 2002 -
  - **Sam** 2004 -

Listening Practice

Listen. Write the answer. ((Track 26))

No, she doesn't.	Just one.	Yes, I am.
My Aunt Janet.	No, it's not that big.	

1. _____
2. _____
3. _____
4. _____
5. _____

Listen. Write the question. ((Track 27))

Does he play golf?	Who are they?	Do they live with you?
How many cousins do you have?	Is she older or younger than you?	

1. _____
2. _____
3. _____
4. _____
5. _____

Describe the picture using the words below.

grandmother children lap youngest

✓ **Listen to the description of the picture.** ((Track 28))

Speaking Practice

Pronunciation Practice

In casual speech, you may hear the word "you" pronounced as "yuh" or "ye," and "your" as "yer."

Written	Spoken
1. How often do you see them?	1. How often do yuh see them?
2. Do you live with your grandparents?	2. Do ye live with yer grandparents?
3. I'd like you to meet my cousin.	3. I'd like ye to meet my cousin.

✓ **Now practice saying the following sentences.**

1. Did you get a chance to talk to my sister?
2. I hope you can visit my grandparents' farm with me.
3. I saw you with your younger brother.

✓ **Now listen and repeat.** (((Track 29)))

B

Conversation Pictures

Listen to the dialogs, and number the pictures. (((Track 30)))

✓ **Now listen to the dialogs again, and choose the correct relationship.**

1. (A) Brothers   (B) Co-workers   (C) Neighbors   (D) Sisters
2. (A) Brothers   (B) Co-workers   (C) Neighbors   (D) Sisters
3. (A) Brothers   (B) Co-workers   (C) Neighbors   (D) Sisters
4. (A) Brothers   (B) Co-workers   (C) Neighbors   (D) Sisters

Short Dialogs

Dialog 1

Listen to the dialog and questions. Choose the best answer. Track 31

1. (A) His aunt   (B) His friend
   (C) His mother   (D) His sister

2. (A) It's small.   (B) It's big.
   (C) It's average.   (D) It's like hers.

✓ **Listen again, and fill in the blanks.**

W: I saw you yesterday in the park. Who was the woman you were with?

M: That was my ❶_____, Catherine.

W: I thought you only had an older brother.

M: Actually, I have an ❷_____ brother and two younger ❸_____.

W: Wow! You've got a big family.

M: Yeah. I guess it's ❹_____ than most families.

Dialog 2

Listen to the dialog and questions. Choose the best answer. Track 32

1. (A) The woman's cousin   (B) The woman's friend
   (C) The woman's in-law   (D) The woman's sister

2. (A) She has a boyfriend.   (B) Her brother is the woman's boyfriend.
   (C) The man is her boyfriend.   (D) Her husband is older than her.

Dialog 3

Listen to the dialog, and write the names in the correct blanks. Track 33

Georgia	Judy	Patrick	Tom

1. _____ is Judy's father.

2. _____ and _____ are married.

Main Dialog

Listen to the dialog, and choose the best answer. ((Track 34))

1. Who gave the woman flowers?
   - (A) Her best friend
   - (B) Her boyfriend
   - (C) Her co-worker
   - (D) Her sister

2. How did the two women meet?
   - (A) Through their parents
   - (B) At work
   - (C) Through friends
   - (D) In school

3. Which is true about the two women?
   - (A) They communicate often.
   - (B) They don't communicate.
   - (C) They rarely communicate.
   - (D) They communicate daily.

Listen again, and fill in the blanks. ((Track 35))

M: The flowers on your desk are very nice. Who sent them to you?

W: Patricia, my ❶_____.

M: I think you've told me about her before. Wasn't she your old ❷_____ friend?

W: Actually, we've known each other since elementary school. So we've been friends for almost ❸_____ years!

M: That's a long ❹_____.

W: Yeah, in some ways I feel like she's almost my ❺_____.

M: Do you two still ❻_____ with each other a lot?

W: Sure. We ❼_____ emails to each other several times a ❽_____.

Short Talks

Short Talk 1

Listen to the short talk and questions. Choose the best answer. ((Track 36))

1. (A) They had a class together.   (B) They lived next to each other.
   (C) They volunteered together.   (D) They were roommates.

2. (A) His friend is older than him.   (B) His friend is younger than him.
   (C) They are the same age.   (D) He does not know his friend's age.

✓ **Listen again, and fill in the blanks.**

My best friend is Michael. We've known each other since
❶_____. We didn't have any classes together
because he is one year ❷_____ than me. I met
him when I ❸_____ to work on the school's
❹_____. He was the school newspaper's
photographer.

Short Talk 2

Listen to the short talk and questions. Choose the best answer. ((Track 37))

1. (A) The woman's children   (B) The woman's friends
   (C) The woman's neighbors   (D) The woman's relatives

2. (A) They don't want children.   (B) They have many children.
   (C) They don't have any children.   (D) They travel with children.

C

Short Talk 3

Listen to the short talk, and match the information that goes together. ((Track 38))

1. Great-grandmother •   • (A) in Arizona

2. The funeral   •   • (B) in Hollywood

3. Cousin Juan   •   • (C) from Mexico

Listening Quiz

04:22

Listen to the dialogs. Choose the correct picture. ((Track 39))

A

B

C

1. (A)   (B)   (C)

2. (A)   (B)   (C)

Listen to the dialogs and questions. Choose the best answer. ((Track 40))

3. (A) Brothers   (B) Co-workers
   (C) Cousins   (D) Friends

4. (A) Her friend   (B) Her nephew
   (C) Her parents   (D) Her sister

5. (A) How old she is   (B) How she looks
   (C) What her job is   (D) Who her boyfriend is

6. (A) His ex-girlfriend   (B) His friend's ex-girlfriend
   (C) His friend's girlfriend   (D) His friend's sister

7. (A) Her brother's   (B) Her grandfather's
   (C) Her father's   (D) Her uncle's

8. (A) Friends and co-workers   (B) Just her grandfather
   (C) Many of her relatives   (D) Only her brothers and sisters

9. (A) He is not alive.   (B) He lives in Vancouver.
   (C) He moved.   (D) He works far away.

Wrap-up

A
Pre-listening Discussion

Talk about these questions.

1. How many children did your grandparents have?
2. How many children do your parents have?
3. How many children would you like to have?

B
Listening Comprehension

Listen and answer the questions. ((Track 41))

1. **How many people were in the average family in the 1950s?**
   In the 1950s, the average family had _____.

2. **How many people does the average family have today?**
   Today, the average family has _____.

3. **How has the size of first homes changed in the United States?**
   In the United States, the size of first homes has _____.

C
Dictation Practice

Listen again, and fill in the blanks. ((Track 42))

In the 1950s, most ❶_____ in the United States included ❷_____ people: two parents and ❸_____ children. Since that time, the ❹_____ of the American family has become ❺_____. In 1970, the average ❻_____ family had only ❼_____ people. In 2000, the average ❽_____ family only had ❾_____ people. That means for every 100 ❿_____ couples, only ⓫_____ couples had ⓬_____. Among the couples with ⓭_____, these parents only had ⓮_____ child. Of course, these ⓯_____ are only for the average ⓰_____. It is true that White, ⓱_____, and Asian families now have ⓲_____ children than in the ⓳_____, but the size of ⓴_____ families has not changed ㉑_____. However, in general it is ㉒_____ today to find a family in ㉓_____ with more than ㉔_____ people, including children.

Although the ㉕_____ of the family has gone ㉖_____ in the United States, the ㉗_____ size of the American ㉘_____ has grown. In 1970, the first ㉙_____ a new family bought was usually ㉚_____ square meters. In ㉛_____, a new family's first ㉜_____ was more than ㉝_____ square meters.

Listening Test ⏱ 08:53

PART I: Picture Description ((Track 43))

Listen and choose the statement that best describes what you see in the picture.

1.

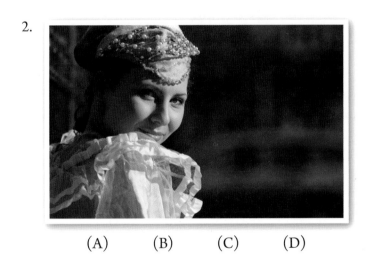

(A)   (B)   (C)   (D)

2.

(A)   (B)   (C)   (D)

3.

(A)   (B)   (C)   (D)

4.

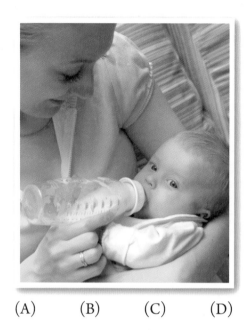

(A)   (B)   (C)   (D)

5.

(A)   (B)   (C)   (D)

PART II: Questions and Responses ((Track 44))

Listen and choose the best response to each question.

6. (A)   (B)   (C)

7. (A)   (B)   (C)

8. (A)   (B)   (C)

9. (A)   (B)   (C)

10. (A)   (B)   (C)

PART III: Short Conversations ((Track 45))

You will hear two dialogs, each followed by three questions. Listen carefully, and choose the best answer to each question.

11. Why did the woman think the house is probably expensive?

    (A) It is too large.
    (B) It has expensive furniture.
    (C) It is in the center of town.
    (D) The man told her.

12. What does the man say is a bad point about the house?

    (A) It has a small yard.
    (B) It is downtown.
    (C) It has many rooms.
    (D) It is too big.

13. Why did the man mention drink spills?

    (A) He noticed some on the carpet.
    (B) He said they would be hard to see on the carpet.
    (C) He had some on his pants.
    (D) He thinks the carpet has a strong color.

---

14. What is the man talking about?

    (A) His mother
    (B) His niece's appearance
    (C) Photographs
    (D) Who is the cutest in his family

15. Who is shown in the picture?

    (A) A teenage boy
    (B) A teenage girl
    (C) A baby boy
    (D) A baby girl

16. What does the woman say about the man?

    (A) He looks like his mother.
    (B) He has a birthday in March.
    (C) His niece is better looking than he is.
    (D) He should smile more.

PART IV: Short Talks ((Track 46))

You will hear two talks, each followed by three questions. Listen carefully, and choose the best answer to each question.

17. What is being advertised?
    (A) A new store
    (B) A television program
    (C) A website
    (D) Lost relatives

18. What can people get from this service?
    (A) Children
    (B) Free gifts
    (C) New friends
    (D) Information

19. What does the advertisement NOT say?
    (A) Sign up for their service
    (B) Go to their website
    (C) Discover previously unknown relatives
    (D) Pay a monthly fee

___

20. Who is Kevin?
    (A) The man's brother
    (B) The man's cousin
    (C) The man's friend
    (D) The man's nephew

21. Which is true about his relationship with Kevin?
    (A) They are in love with the same girl.
    (B) They did not like each other for many years.
    (C) They do not know each other well.
    (D) They have known each other for many years.

22. Where is this speech being given?
    (A) At a business meeting
    (B) At a political conference
    (C) At a company picnic
    (D) At a wedding reception

UNIT 3 Free Time

Warm-up

A Look & Listen

Listen to the dialogs. (((Track 47)))

B Listen Again

Listen again, and match the activity with the time. (((Track 48)))

1. collecting •
2. reading •
3. in-line skating •
4. playing guitar •

• (A) years ago
• (B) last year
• (C) now
• (D) in the future

C Essential Expressions

Circle the best word or phrase to complete each question.

1. Can you (play / to play) tennis?
2. Do you enjoy (playing / to play) the guitar?
3. How long have you been (collect / collecting) stamps?
4. What do you like (cook / to cook)?
5. Do you like (read / to read)?
6. How do you usually (spend time / to spend time) on weekends?
7. What kind of movies do you (enjoy / enjoying)?
8. How often do you (paint / painting)?
9. What movie did you (see / seeing) last weekend?
10. Where do you like (hang out / hanging out)?

Listening Practice

How would you answer?

Listen. Write the answer. ((Track 49))

No, I'm not.	Not very well.	Sure, that's fine.
Yes, I do.	Two or three times a month.	

1. _____
2. _____
3. _____
4. _____
5. _____

B

How would you ask?

Listen. Write the question. ((Track 50))

Do you enjoy cooking?   Can you ice skate?   How often do you play tennis?
Do you have any plans for this weekend?   What do you like to do in your free time?

1. _____
2. _____
3. _____
4. _____
5. _____

C

Picture Description

Describe the picture using the words below.

flowers	trowel	wear	hold

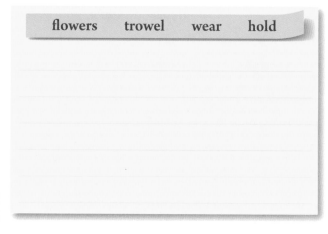

✓ **Listen to the description of the picture.** ((Track 51))

Speaking Practice

Pronunciation Practice

In casual speech, you may hear the word "can" pronounced as "kin."

Written	Spoken
1. What songs can you play on the guitar?	1. What songs kin you play on the guitar?
2. We can do something on Sunday afternoon.	2. We kin do something on Sunday afternoon.
3. You can read a book if you're bored.	3. You kin read a book if you're bored.

✓ **Now practice saying the following sentences.**

1. Can you draw people well?
2. My sister can beat anyone at chess.
3. What can we do tonight after dinner?

✓ **Now listen and repeat.** ((Track 52))

B Conversation Pictures

Listen to the dialogs, and number the pictures. ((Track 53))

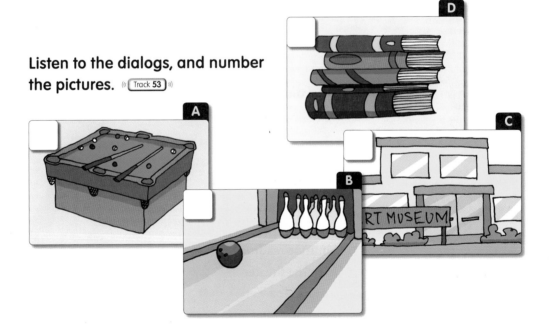

✓ **Now listen to the dialogs again, and choose the correct time of each activity.**

1. (A) Past   (B) Present   (C) Future
2. (A) Past   (B) Present   (C) Future
3. (A) Past   (B) Present   (C) Future
4. (A) Past   (B) Present   (C) Future

Short Dialogs

A

Dialog 1

Listen to the dialog and questions. Choose the best answer. ((Track 54))

1. (A) A library   (B) A park
   (C) A place for exercising   (D) A place with stores

2. (A) Playing music   (B) Watching videos
   (C) Looking around   (D) Working out

✓ **Listen again, and fill in the blanks.**

W: What do you like to do in your free time?

M: I like to hang out at ❶_____.

W: Really? I didn't know you liked ❷_____ so much.

M: I don't shop. I spend most of my time playing ❸_____ or just window shopping in bookstores or ❹_____ stores.

B

Dialog 2

Listen to the dialog and questions. Choose the best answer. ((Track 55))

1. (A) A drama
   (B) A romantic comedy
   (C) A horror movie
   (D) An action movie

2. (A) Continue reading
   (B) Go to the theater
   (C) Rent a video
   (D) Talk to the man

C

Dialog 3

Listen to the dialog, and complete the sentences. ((Track 56))

1. The male speaker plays the _____.

2. His sister plays the _____.

Main Dialog

Listen to the dialog, and choose the best answer. ((Track 57))

1. What is the man's hobby?
   - (A) Driving
   - (B) Reading books
   - (C) Sailing boats
   - (D) Working on his car

2. Which is true about the man?
   - (A) He has more than one car.
   - (B) He is a mechanic.
   - (C) His wife does not drive.
   - (D) His car is not very good.

3. How does her grandfather feel about boats?
   - (A) He ignores them.
   - (B) He likes them a lot.
   - (C) They make him mad.
   - (D) They need a lot of work.

Listen again, and fill in the blanks. ((Track 58))

W: You look busy.

M: I was cleaning my car engine.

W: I see you working on your car ❶_____.

M: I guess it's my ❷_____.

W: How can that be your hobby?

M: I like reading books about ❸_____ care and buying parts for my car.

W: Do you ever ❹_____ your car?

M: This car is only for ❺_____ drives in the country. My wife and I drive our other car only around in the city.

W: You ❻_____ me of my grandfather.

M: What's his hobby?

W: ❼_____ and taking care of boats. He ❽_____ sailboats.

Short Talks

Listen to the short talk and questions. Choose the best answer. ((Track 59))

1. (A) At night   (B) In the morning
   (C) On Friday   (D) On weekends

2. (A) Goes to movies   (B) Meets her friends
   (C) Reads books   (D) Watches television

✓ **Listen again, and fill in the blanks.**

I have a lot of homework every day. But I can still enjoy a little free time ❶_____. After dinner, I usually watch television for ❷_____ before I start working on my homework. These days, I enjoy watching a ❸_____ about three women ❹_____ together in a house in Los Angeles.

Listen to the short talk and questions. Choose the best answer. ((Track 60))

1. (A) He has to work.   (B) He has two jobs.
   (C) His apartment is large.   (D) His parents visit him.

2. (A) An hour each night   (B) Two full days
   (C) Only one day   (D) None

Listen to the short talk, and list three things that each person collects. ((Track 61))

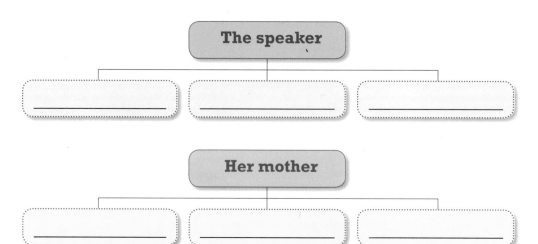

The speaker

_____   _____   _____

Her mother

_____   _____   _____

**Picture
Matching**

Listen to the dialogs. Choose the correct picture. ((Track 62))

1. (A)   (B)   (C)

2. (A)   (B)   (C)

Listen & Choose

Listen to the dialogs and questions. Choose the best answer. ((Track 63))

3. (A) Collecting beds   (B) Collecting boxes
   (C) Collecting postcards   (D) Collecting stamps

4. (A) See animals   (B) Travel
   (C) Visit his parents   (D) Watch a movie

5. (A) Plays a sport   (B) Studies
   (C) Tutors other students   (D) Works at a store

6. (A) He does not like TV.   (B) He rarely watches TV.
   (C) He should buy a TV.   (D) He watches TV a lot.

7. (A) Movies and sports   (B) Music shows and news
   (C) News and movies   (D) Sports and music shows

8. (A) Chinese   (B) French
   (C) Italian   (D) Middle Eastern

9. (A) Help him   (B) Go away
   (C) Let him cook   (D) Order some food

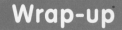

Wrap-up

A

Pre-listening Discussion

Talk about these questions.

1. How much free time do you have each day? On weekends?
2. In general, who has more free time, men or women?
3. What do you do in your free time?

B

Listening Comprehension

Listen and answer the questions. ((Track 64))

1. **How long did the researchers do this study?**
   The researchers did this study for _____.

2. **Who has more free time, Australian men or women?**
   _____ have more free time than _____.

3. **What is the most popular free time activity for Australians?**
   The most popular free time activity for Australians is _____.

C

Dictation Practice

Researchers in Australia wanted to ❶_____ out how people spent their ❷_____ time. The researchers asked people to ❸_____ down all of the ❹_____ they had done for two ❺_____.

Through the survey, most ❻_____ said they had between ❼_____ and five hours of free ❽_____ each day during the ❾_____. On weekends, they had between ❿_____ and seven hours of ⓫_____ time. In comparing the free ⓬_____ available to men and women, the ⓭_____ found that men had a little ⓮_____ free time than women. This was ⓯_____ because women spend more time ⓰_____ housework and taking care of ⓱_____.

During the two-day research period, ⓲_____ percent of the people taking the ⓳_____ said they spent time ⓴_____ TV or videos. 75 percent said they ㉑_____ time socializing with family or ㉒_____. 57 percent said they spent time ㉓_____ to music, and 48 percent spent time ㉔_____. Only 27 percent said they played ㉕_____ or exercised, and less than ㉖_____ percent watched a sporting ㉗_____. It was also found that ㉘_____ often did more than ㉙_____ free-time activity at the ㉚_____ time. For example, many people ㉛_____ socializing as their free time ㉜_____, but they also mentioned watching ㉝_____ at the same time.

PART I: Picture Description ((Track 66))

Listen and choose the statement that best describes what you see in the picture.

1.

(A)   (B)   (C)   (D)

2.

(A)   (B)   (C)   (D)

3.

(A)   (B)   (C)   (D)

4.

(A)   (B)   (C)   (D)

5.

(A)   (B)   (C)   (D)

PART II: Questions and Responses ((Track 67))

Listen and choose the best response to each question.

6. (A)   (B)   (C)

7. (A)   (B)   (C)

8. (A)   (B)   (C)

9. (A)   (B)   (C)

10. (A)   (B)   (C)

PART III: Short Conversations ((Track 68))

You will hear two dialogs, each followed by three questions. Listen carefully, and choose the best answer to each question.

11. What event is the couple attending?

    (A) A horror movie

    (B) A play

    (C) A concert

    (D) A documentary

12. Where will they sit?

    (A) Above the stage

    (B) Behind the stage

    (C) Near the stage

    (D) On the stage

13. How does the woman feel about their seats?

    (A) She wants to hurry up and find them.

    (B) They seem far away.

    (C) She wants to move closer.

    (D) She doesn't want to sit down.

---

14. What does the woman say about golf?

    (A) It is a great sport.

    (B) She does not understand why people like it.

    (C) She already knows how the game is played.

    (D) She wants to learn how to play it.

15. Which is true of the opinions of the woman and the man?

    (A) They agree.

    (B) They don't agree.

    (C) They have no opinion.

    (D) They are joking.

16. What does the man say about shopping?

    (A) He wants to go shopping soon.

    (B) He gets bored when he shops for clothes.

    (C) He doesn't like shopping for clothes with the woman.

    (D) He agrees with her opinion about shopping.

PART IV: Short Talks ((Track 69))

You will hear two talks, each followed by three questions. Listen carefully, and choose the best answer to each question.

17. What does the announcement want people to register?

 (A) A work of art
 (B) A science project
 (C) A speech
 (D) Their name for a study course

18. What will the winner of the contest receive?

 (A) A painting
 (B) A trip to Paris
 (C) Money
 (D) Nothing

19. Where will the event take place?

 (A) At a local high school
 (B) November 1st
 (C) At a country fair
 (D) At a museum

---

20. What is the main subject of the announcement?

 (A) Suggestions for a good job interview
 (B) Inappropriate interview questions
 (C) How to ask questions
 (D) The law in the United States

21. Which interview question is considered illegal in the US?

 (A) Do you have any plans for the weekend?
 (B) Do you have any hobbies?
 (C) How old are you?
 (D) Why are you applying for this job?

22. Which of the following statements was made in the announcement?

 (A) Go to the police if you hear an illegal job interview question.
 (B) Most interview questions make applicants uncomfortable.
 (C) Sometimes an interview question can be funny.
 (D) Some job interview questions can make applicants uncomfortable.

4 Date and Time

Warm-up

A

Look & Listen

Listen to the dialogs. ((Track 70))

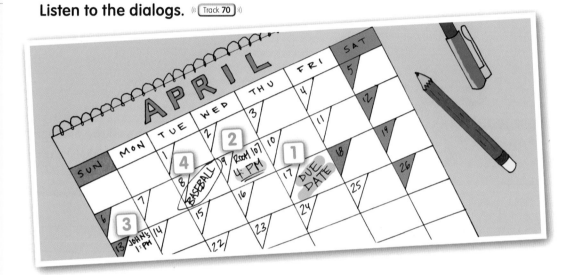

Listen Again

B

Listen again, and fill in the blanks. ((Track 71))

1. There is _____ due on Thursday the 17th.
2. The _____ meeting will start at four o'clock on Wednesday.
3. Over the weekend, she will be busy on _____, but she is free on _____.
4. According to the calendar, today is _____ April _____th.

Essential Expressions

C

Circle the correct word.

1. I don't have any plans (next / on) weekend.
2. Let's meet at the library (at / in) 6:30 tonight.
3. He usually gets home (around / to) 4:30 each day.
4. She said the meeting will finish (by / on) five o'clock.
5. The homework assignment is due (at / on) Friday.
6. In Canada, Thanksgiving is always the second Monday (at / of) October.
7. The movie will start (in / on) ten minutes.
8. Isn't there a holiday (at / on) the 15th of this month?
9. Our school will be closed (from / on) Thursday until next Tuesday.
10. Which day will the test be (in / on)?

Listening Practice

A

How would you answer?

Listen. Write the answer. ((Track 72))

At 7:30.	How about 5:30?	No, we're not.
Not until the 15th.	Tuesday.	

1. _____

2. _____

3. _____

4. _____

5. _____

B

How would you ask?

Listen. Write the question. ((Track 73))

What time will it arrive?	When will the package be delivered?
When do you want to meet?	Which day is best for you?
Which day is the concert on?	

1. _____

2. _____

3. _____

4. _____

5. _____

C

Picture Description

Describe the picture using the words below.

chart	draw	explain	office

_____

_____

_____

_____

_____

✓ **Listen to the description of the picture.** ((Track 74))

Speaking Practice

A
Intonation
Practice

In certain two-syllable statements or questions, the stress will usually be on the first syllable. Study these two-syllable statements and questions that have the first syllable stressed.

Written	Spoken
1. Tuesday.	1. **Tues**day.
2. No, thanks.	2. **No**, thanks.
3. Thanks, Joe.	3. **Thanks**, Joe.

✓ **Now practice saying the following sentences. Remember to stress the first syllable.**

1. That's right.
2. Not bad.
3. Not much.

✓ **Now listen and repeat.** ((Track 75))

B
Conversation
Pictures

Listen to the dialogs, and number the pictures. ((Track 76))

✓ **Now listen to the dialogs again, and choose the correct day.**

1. (A) Monday (B) Wednesday (C) Thursday (D) Saturday
2. (A) Monday (B) Wednesday (C) Thursday (D) Saturday
3. (A) Monday (B) Wednesday (C) Thursday (D) Saturday
4. (A) Monday (B) Wednesday (C) Thursday (D) Saturday

Short Dialogs

Dialog 1

Listen to the dialog and questions. Choose the best answer. ((Track 77))

1. (A) The man's   (B) The woman's
   (C) The man's brother's   (D) The woman's sister's

2. (A) On a weekday   (B) On a weeknight
   (C) On a weekend afternoon   (D) On a Sunday evening

✓ **Listen again, and fill in the blanks.**

W: When is your brother's birthday party?

M: It's on the 19th.

W: Great! The 19th is a ❶_____ this month.

M: Right. So the party is going to start early in the afternoon.

W: What time will the party ❷_____?

M: My ❸_____ told everyone to come over around ❹_____ o'clock.

Dialog 2

Listen to the dialog and questions. Choose the best answer. ((Track 78))

1. (A) She has a class.   (B) She is going shopping.
   (C) She is working.   (D) She does not say.

2. (A) At her house   (B) At his house
   (C) At the bus stop   (D) At the theater

Dialog 3

Listen to the dialog, and write the day of the week that goes with each phrase. ((Track 79))

Sunday	Monday	Tuesday	Wednesday	Thursday	Friday

1. The holiday starts: _____

2. The holiday ends: _____

Main Dialog

A

Listen

Listen to the dialog, and choose the best answer. ((Track 80))

1. What will they do when they meet?
   - (A) Have dinner
   - (B) Look for a book
   - (C) See a movie
   - (D) Study

2. Why can't she meet on Wednesday?
   - (A) She has a class.
   - (B) She will be in a game.
   - (C) She works in the library.
   - (D) She has to cook dinner.

3. When will they meet?
   - (A) In the morning
   - (B) At noon
   - (C) Late in the afternoon
   - (D) At night

B

Listen Again

Listen again, and fill in the blanks. ((Track 81))

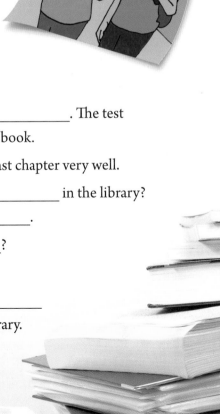

M: Let's study for the test together.

W: Sure, I'd love to.

M: Can we get together ❶_____ this week?

W: I have a soccer game on Wednesday night. How about ❷_____?

M: Great. What time?

W: We should meet ❸_____. The test covers three chapters from the book.

M: Yeah, I didn't understand the last chapter very well.

W: Why don't we meet at ❹_____ in the library? We can stay until ❺_____.

M: What about ❻_____?

W: Let's just bring some snacks.

M: Alright, I'll see you ❼_____ at ❽_____ in the library.

W: Great. See you then.

Short Talks

Listen to the short talk and questions. Choose the best answer. (((Track 82)))

1. (A) He is in the wrong place.   (B) He remembered the wrong time.
   (C) Jeff did not get his call.   (D) Jeff forgot the date.

2. (A) Buy a ticket   (B) Call Jeff's cell phone
   (C) Leave   (D) Stay a short time more

✓ **Listen again, and fill in the blanks.**

Hi, Jeff. This is Nelson. I was just ❶_____ to see if you were there. I'm here at the stadium near the north ticket windows. I thought we were supposed to meet here at ❷_____, but maybe I had the wrong ❸_____ in mind. If you get this message, ❹_____ me a call on my cell phone. Otherwise, I guess I'll wait for 30 minutes to see if you show up. Bye.

Listen to the short talk and questions. Choose the best answer. (((Track 83)))

1. (A) At a train station   (B) In an airport
   (C) On a tour bus   (D) On an airplane

2. (A) Bad weather   (B) No fuel
   (C) Engine problems   (D) Bad food

Listen to the recording, and write T for true or F for false for each statement. (((Track 84)))

1. _____ The recording asks the caller to hold for an operator.

2. _____ The customer service line opens before 9:00 in the morning.

3. _____ The recording informs the caller of the bank's website.

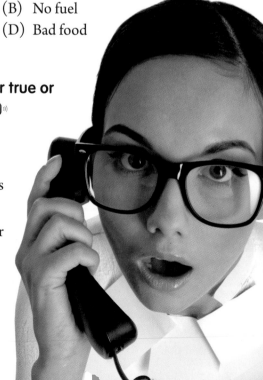

Listening Quiz

04:10

A
Picture Matching

Listen to the dialogs. Choose the correct picture. (((Track 85)))

1. (A)   (B)   (C)

2. (A)   (B)   (C)

B
Listen & Choose

Listen to the dialogs and questions. Choose the best answer. (((Track 86)))

3. (A) He works late.   (B) He does not like tennis.
   (C) He will be tired.   (D) He eats dinner late.

4. (A) About ten minutes   (B) Less than an hour and a half
   (C) More than two hours   (D) All day

5. (A) She will eat dinner.   (B) The meeting will be short.
   (C) They will be tired.   (D) The streets will be busy.

6. (A) Buy his ticket   (B) Have coffee
   (C) Meet Steve   (D) Pick her up

7. (A) At his office   (B) At a coffee shop downtown
   (C) At home   (D) At the airport

8. (A) At noon   (B) In the afternoon
   (C) In the evening   (D) At midnight

9. (A) He is busy.   (B) His friend will come.
   (C) The bakery is large.   (D) The movie is popular.

Wrap-up

A
Pre-listening Discussion

Talk about these questions.

1. Do you like to make plans to use your time wisely?
2. Are you the kind of person who is usually on time or late for appointments?
3. Do you know anyone who is the opposite way? Who?

B
Listening Comprehension

Listen and answer the questions. ((Track 87))

1. **What are the two prefixes defined in the reading? What do they mean?**
   The prefixes are _____, which means _____, and _____, which
   means _____.

2. **Which view of time probably does NOT follow exact schedules?**
   The _____ view of time probably does not follow exact schedules.

3. **Where would things like daily planners sell better, North America or South America?**
   Daily planners would sell better in _____.

C
Dictation Practice

Listen again, and fill in the blanks. ((Track 88))

Did you know that some ❶_____ think about time differently
❷_____ others? They don't ❸_____ clocks differently. They just
❹_____ the importance of time in ❺_____ ways.
    Western cultures like ❻_____ and the United States have a
❼_____ view of time. The prefix "❽_____" means "one," so these
❾_____ think there is only ❿_____ time, and everyone must
⓫_____ that time. For these ⓬_____, it is very important
to ⓭_____ things at the proper ⓮_____. They hate being
late for ⓯_____. They also think ⓰_____ can be lost or
⓱_____, so it must be used ⓲_____.
    Other cultures (for example, ⓳_____ cultures in South
American) have a ⓴_____ view of time. The prefix
"㉑_____" means "many," so these ㉒_____ think things
happen according ㉓_____ their own times. For these
㉔_____, time is flexible and other ㉕_____ may be more
important than ㉖_____ a strict schedule. In a ㉗_____,
people from these cultures ㉘_____ want to take time for
㉙_____. They think it is ㉚_____ to build a relationship
㉛_____ others before starting ㉜_____.

Listening Test 🕗 08:37

PART I: Picture Description (((Track 89)))

Listen and choose the statement that best describes what you see in the picture.

1.

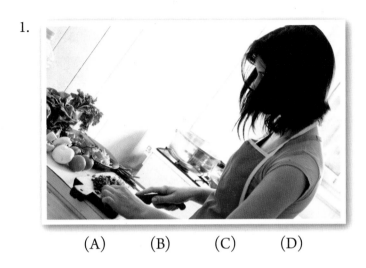

    (A)   (B)   (C)   (D)

2.

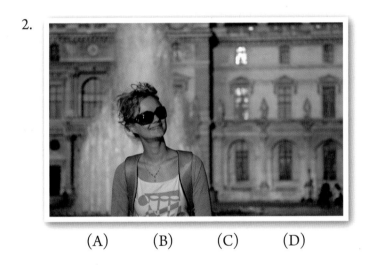

    (A)   (B)   (C)   (D)

3.

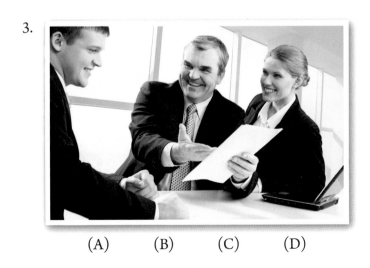

    (A)   (B)   (C)   (D)

4.

(A).   (B)   (C)   (D)

5.

(A)   (B)   (C)   (D)

PART II: Questions and Responses ((Track 90))

Listen and choose the best response to each question.

6. (A)   (B)   (C)

7. (A)   (B)   (C)

8. (A)   (B)   (C)

9. (A)   (B)   (C)

10. (A)   (B)   (C)

PART III: Short Conversations (((Track 91)))

You will hear two dialogs, each followed by three questions. Listen carefully, and choose the best answer to each question.

11. Where does this conversation take place?

    (A) In a taxi
    (B) In an airplane
    (C) On a boat
    (D) On a bus

12. What does the woman's last statement mean?

    (A) They are going to the beach.
    (B) They are going to the hotel first.
    (C) They are going to be late to the meeting.
    (D) They are going to enjoy their vacation.

13. What was the captain able to do?

    (A) Land fifteen minutes early
    (B) Answer the passengers' questions
    (C) Depart late
    (D) Get back on schedule after the plane departed late

---

14. What does the woman do on weekends?

    (A) She does some work around the house.
    (B) She makes an appointment.
    (C) She meets the man.
    (D) She see a doctor.

15. What did the man first ask the woman?

    (A) If she was busy on Saturday
    (B) If she works on weekends
    (C) If she relaxes on the weekends
    (D) If she makes rules

16. What does the woman do on Sundays?

    (A) Works an extra job
    (B) Meets friends
    (C) Plays tennis
    (D) Does her household chores

PART IV: Short Talks ((Track 92))

You will hear two talks, each followed by three questions. Listen carefully, and choose the best answer to each question.

17. What does this announcement explain?

    (A) A guest speaker at the conference
    (B) How to sign up for the conference
    (C) The new conference schedule
    (D) Where the conference will be held

18. How many people will speak at two o'clock?

    (A) None
    (B) One
    (C) Two
    (D) Three

19. Which has changed for the networking seminar?

    (A) The location
    (B) The speaker
    (C) The time
    (D) The title

---

20. What is being described?

    (A) A bus schedule
    (B) A school's schedule
    (C) A special trip
    (D) An unusual morning

21. Which of the following did he NOT do?

    (A) Come to his first class late
    (B) Take a quiz
    (C) Miss the bus
    (D) Sleep late

22. What happened to him at home?

    (A) He had breakfast.
    (B) He woke up late.
    (C) He left on time.
    (D) He took the next bus.

Telephone

Warm-up

A
Look & Listen

Listen to the dialogs. ((Track 93))

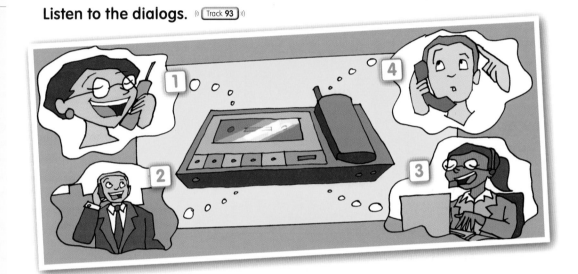

B
Listen Again

Listen again, and fill in the blanks. ((Track 94))

1. His mother called about meeting Tom for _____ on _____.
2. Andrew called about meeting Tom at _____ tonight around _____.
3. Good Rates Travel Service called about a special _____ on trips to _____.
4. Someone called looking for _____, but it was a _____ number.

C
Essential Expressions

Write the missing words to make correct expressions.

call	direct	expect	got	help
isn't	leave	stay	take	try

1. How may I _____ your call ?
2. Please _____ on the line.
3. I'll _____ again a little later.
4. May I _____ you?
5. Please _____ back during our regular office hours.
6. Ms. Jones is out of the office. Can I _____ a message?
7. Would you like to _____ a message?
8. I think I've _____ the wrong number.
9. He _____ here at the moment.
10. When do you _____ him back?

Listening Practice

A

How would you answer?

Listen. Write the answer. ((Track 95))

> No. No message.   Yes, I would. Please tell her Jane called.   Hello.
> This is his friend, Ray.   Yes, please. Have her call me at home.

1. _____
2. _____
3. _____
4. _____
5. _____

B

How would you ask?

Listen. Write the question. ((Track 96))

> Can I take a message?   May I have your phone number?
> Who is this?   May I help you?   Can you hear me?

1. _____
2. _____
3. _____
4. _____
5. _____

C

Picture Description

Describe the picture using the words below.

desk	look	laptop	hold

✓ **Listen to the description of the picture.** ((Track 97))

Speaking Practice

Pronunciation
Practice

In casual speech, you may hear the word "your" or "you're" pronounced as "yer."

Written	Spoken
1. Is this your home phone number?	1. Is this yer home phone number?
2. I'll give him your name and number.	2. I'll give him yer name and number.
3. You're welcome.	3. Yer welcome.

✓ **Now practice saying the following sentences.**

1. Your sister called this morning.
2. You're going to call back later, right?
3. Did you say you're meeting them at noon?

✓ **Now listen and repeat.** ((Track 98))

B

Conversation
Pictures

Listen to the dialogs, and number the pictures. ((Track 99))

✓ **Now listen to the messages again, and choose the correct message.**

1. (A) Call me.   (B) I'll call again.   (C) I'll meet you later.
2. (A) Call me.   (B) I'll call again.   (C) I'll meet you later.
3. (A) Call me.   (B) I'll call again.   (C) I'll meet you later.
4. (A) Call me.   (B) I'll call again.   (C) I'll meet you later.

Short Dialogs

A

Dialog 1

Listen to the dialog and questions. Choose the best answer. ((Track 100))

1. (A) He went to the park.   (B) He went to school.
   (C) He went to work.   (D) She does not say.

2. (A) He can't meet Joe.   (B) He will call again.
   (C) Joe will be late.   (D) Joe should call him.

✓ **Listen again, and fill in the blanks.**

W: Hello?

M: Hi. Is Joe there?

W: No, he's not ❶_____ at the moment. Can I take a message?

M: Yes, please. ❷_____ you tell him to call Steve when he ❸_____ home?

W: Sure. I'll ❹_____ him the message.

M: Thanks. Bye.

B

Dialog 2

Listen to the dialog and questions. Choose the best answer. ((Track 101))

1. (A) To call a friend   (B) To eat
   (C) To meet someone   (D) To take pictures

2. (A) Immediately   (B) In about 20 minutes
   (C) In an hour   (D) He doesn't know.

C

Dialog 3

Listen to the dialog, and complete each statement. ((Track 102))

1. The woman who is speaking _____
   _____.

2. Someone else_____
   _____.

Main Dialog

A

Listen

Listen to the dialog, and choose the best answer. ((Track 103))

1. What is Bill probably doing?
   (A) Buying something   (B) Exercising
   (C) Fixing his car   (D) Studying

2. What kind of club does Bill belong to?
   (A) A drama club   (B) An English club
   (C) A music club   (D) A sports club

3. Which is true about the club?
   (A) A new member will join.   (B) A meeting date has changed.
   (C) It will have a party soon. (D) Bill is now the president of it.

B

Listen Again

Listen again, and fill in the blanks. ((Track 104))

W: Hello?

M: Hello. Is Bill there?

W: Bill went to the ❶_____, but he'll be
   back soon. Can you call back in about
   ❷_____ minutes?

M: Could you just give him a message for me, ❸_____?

W: Sure. What's the message?

M: The tennis club is not going to
   meet this ❹_____.
   So our next meeting is going to be
   on ❺_____ the 24ᵗʰ.

W: No meeting this ❻_____.
   Next meeting is the 24ᵗʰ. ❼_____ it?

M: That's all.

W: OK, I'll make sure he gets
   the message when he
   ❽_____.

M: Thanks. Bye.

W: Bye.

Short Talks

Listen to the short talk and questions. Choose the best answer. ((Track 105))

1. (A) A movie theater   (B) A restaurant
   (C) A sports center   (D) A video game store

2. (A) Push number one   (B) Push number two
   (C) Push number three   (D) Hold the line

✓ **Listen again, and fill in the blanks.**

Thank you for calling Multiplex ❶_____
Center. For information on today's shows and show
times, press one. For ticket prices and the
❷_____ of this theater, press two. For all
other questions, press three and your call will be transferred
to a ❸_____ manager. To hear these selections
again, please stay on the ❹_____.

Listen to the short talk and questions. Choose the best answer. ((Track 106))

1. (A) A home   (B) An office
   (C) A school   (D) A store

2. (A) Furniture   (B) Sports equipment
   (C) Clothes   (D) Baby animals

Listen to the short talk, and check (✓) the correct person for each phrase. ((Track 107))

	The speaker	Martin
1. Is not at home at the moment	☐	☐
2. Called yesterday	☐	☐

A

Picture Matching

Listen to the dialogs. Choose the correct picture. ((Track 108))

A

B

C

1. (A)   (B)   (C)

2. (A)   (B)   (C)

B

Listen & Choose

Listen to the dialogs and questions. Choose the best answer. ((Track 109))

3. (A) Mary is busy.   (B) Mary answered the phone.
   (C) Mary is out.   (D) The man does not know Mary.

4. (A) A house   (B) A school
   (C) A store   (D) A wrong number

5. (A) Call Shelly ASAP.   (B) Your friend Shelly called.
   (C) Meet Shelly at school.   (D) Shelly is at school.

6. (A) Harry called him.   (B) Harry didn't meet him.
   (C) Joe is bored.   (D) Joe is late.

7. (A) Joe called.   (B) Joe is sorry.
   (C) Joe needs help.   (D) Joe won't be there.

8. (A) A man called.   (B) A saleswoman will call later.
   (C) A woman called.   (D) William got a message.

9. (A) Meet William   (B) Look for a phone number
   (C) Call William   (D) Wait for the man to call

Wrap-up

Talk about these questions.

1. What do you say when you answer the phone in your country? What does this mean in English?
2. Do you mind if people call you late at night or early in the morning?
3. What kind of phone technology is popular in your country these days?

Listen and answer the questions. ((Track 110))

1. **After what time in the evening should you not call someone in Canada?**
   You should not call someone in Canada after _____.

2. **Why should you consider the Canadian time zones when you call someone?**
   You should consider Canadian time zones when you call someone because
   _____.

3. **What suggestion does the speaker give if you have to leave a message on a machine?**
   The speaker suggests _____
   if you have to leave a message on a machine.

Listen again, and fill in the blanks. ((Track 111))

    Here are some polite ❶_____ to follow when calling ❷_____ in Canada. If you are the ❸_____, say "hello" and give your ❹_____ when the person answers the ❺_____.

    Another good rule to ❻_____ in mind is that you should ❼_____ call too early or too ❽_____. People in Canada respect ❾_____ other's privacy, and this ❿_____ their home life. If you ⓫_____ someone before ⓬_____ in the morning or after ⓭_____ at night, it could ⓮_____ them or wake them up. ⓯_____, remember Canada is a big ⓰_____. There are several different ⓱_____ zones across the country, so ⓲_____ the time you are ⓳_____ carefully to make sure it is ⓴_____ too early or too ㉑_____ for the person you ㉒_____ calling.

    Many people in ㉓_____ have answering machines to ㉔_____ phone messages for them. It is ㉕_____ to leave a short ㉖_____, even if it is just ㉗_____ name and to say that you ㉘_____ call again later. If you ㉙_____ there is a good chance ㉚_____ will have to leave a ㉛_____ on a machine, you can ㉜_____ down your message before you ㉝_____. This will help you ㉞_____ a clearer message.

Listening Test 🕘 09:00

PART I: Picture Description ((Track 112))

Listen and choose the statement that best describes what you see in the picture.

1.

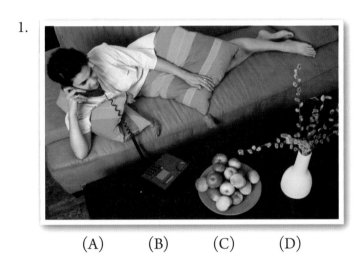

(A)   (B)   (C)   (D)

2.

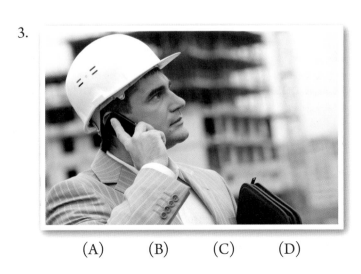

(A)   (B)   (C)   (D)

3.

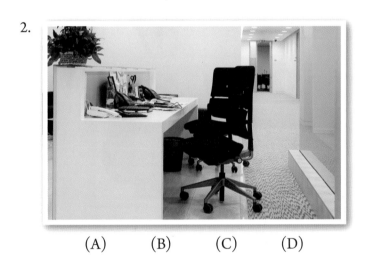

(A)   (B)   (C)   (D)

4.

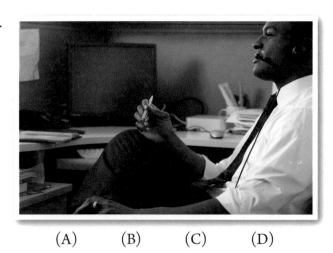

(A)   (B)   (C)   (D)

5.

(A)   (B)   (C)   (D)

PART II: Questions and Responses ((Track 113))

Listen and choose the best response to each question.

6. (A)   (B)   (C)

7. (A)   (B)   (C)

8. (A)   (B)   (C)

9. (A)   (B)   (C)

10. (A)   (B)   (C)

PART III: Short Conversations ((Track 114))

You will hear two dialogs, each followed by three questions. Listen carefully, and choose the best answer to each question.

11. What did the woman want to know?

 (A) Who left the message
 (B) Who was going to take calls
 (C) Who was the customer
 (D) Who wrote down the message

12. What problem did they have?

 (A) They didn't have the customer's address.
 (B) They didn't know what the caller ID was.
 (C) They didn't like Mary.
 (D) They didn't have the customer's phone number.

13. What was the woman's response to the man's suggestion?

 (A) She didn't like it.
 (B) She liked it, but wanted to have lunch first.
 (C) She liked it, but wanted to ask Mary a question.
 (D) She thought the man should check again.

---

14. What was true about the man who called?

 (A) He was at home.
 (B) He wasn't at home.
 (C) He needed to get some information.
 (D) He wanted to speak more to the woman.

15. What did the woman need?

 (A) Something to write with
 (B) Something to write on
 (C) A chair
 (D) A new phone number

16. What was the man's final response?

 (A) He'll wait for the person to return his call.
 (B) He'd like to meet the person somewhere.
 (C) He'll give another call at a later time.
 (D) He'll stop by to say hello.

PART IV: Short Talks ((Track 115))

You will hear two talks, each followed by three questions. Listen carefully, and choose the best answer to each question.

17. Where was the caller probably trying to reach?

    (A) A hospital
    (B) A music store
    (C) A theater
    (D) A video store

18. What information is NOT provided in the message?

    (A) Location
    (B) Prices
    (C) Times of operation
    (D) Title of show

19. What request did the message make?

    (A) Call back to reserve seats
    (B) Hurry to the show
    (C) Come to a special show on Saturday
    (D) Press a button

---

20. Which might be an extension at this office?

    (A) 4
    (B) 42
    (C) 424
    (D) 4242

21. What is implied about speaking to a customer service representative?

    (A) Representatives do not work at night.
    (B) The company has only one.
    (C) The representative is taking a break.
    (D) There may be a wait.

22. Which of the following is true about the message?

    (A) The message is a recording.
    (B) The person speaking is a secretary.
    (C) The caller is asked to leave a message.
    (D) The message automatically forwards you to a representative.

6 Directions

Warm-up

A
Look & Listen

Listen to the dialogs. ((Track 116))

B
Listen Again

Listen again, and fill in the blanks. ((Track 117))

1. The man is looking for the _____.
2. The woman is looking for the nearest _____.
3. The law office is on the _____ floor.
4. There is a _____ two blocks down the street.

C
Essential Expressions

Circle the correct phrase for each question.

1. Which is closer?
   (A) Something a few blocks away   (B) Something one block down

2. Which is a greater distance?
   (A) Far away   (B) Not much further

3. Which one is something you can see?
   (A) Something just around the corner   (B) Something right over there

4. Which one means "go and then stop"?
   (A) Go straight ahead   (B) Go until you reach it

5. Which one tells the direction to go?
   (A) Heading north   (B) The nearest one

Listening Practice

A
How would you answer?

Listen. Write the answer. ((Track 118))

> Yes, it is.   I think there is one by the bank.   Yes, I am.
> No, I don't.   It's that street where the traffic light is.

1. _____
2. _____
3. _____
4. _____
5. _____

B
How would you ask?

Listen. Write the question. ((Track 119))

> Can I buy a map anywhere around here?
> Where can I find men's shoes?   Do you know where City Hall is?
> Should I turn here?   Where is the elevator?

1. _____
2. _____
3. _____
4. _____
5. _____

C
Picture Description

Describe the picture using the words below.

backpack	map	tree	stick

✓ **Listen to the description of the picture.** ((Track 120))

Speaking Practice

A

Pronunciation Practice

In casual speech, you may hear the word "to" pronounced as "tuh."

Written	Spoken
1. I'm trying to find the nearest bakery.	1. I'm trying tuh find the nearest bakery.
2. How can I get to City Hall from here?	2. How kin I get tuh City Hall from here?
3. It's next to the elevators.	3. It's next tuh the elevators.

✓ **Now practice saying the following sentences.**

1. This highway will take you to the airport.
2. If you get to the stoplight, you went too far.
3. I was just about to head over to your house.

✓ **Now listen and repeat.** ((Track 121))

B

Conversation Pictures

Listen to the dialogs, and number the pictures. ((Track 122))

✓ **Now listen to the dialogs again, and choose where the person is going.**

1. (A) A classroom   (B) A gate   (C) A town   (D) A university
2. (A) A classroom   (B) A gate   (C) A town   (D) A university
3. (A) A classroom   (B) A gate   (C) A town   (D) A university
4. (A) A classroom   (B) A gate   (C) A town   (D) A university

Short Dialogs

A

Dialog 1

Listen to the dialog and questions. Choose the best answer. ((Track 123))

1. (A) The restroom   (B) The elevator
   (C) The escalator   (D) The toy department

2. (A) In another store   (B) On another floor
   (C) On the same floor   (D) Outside the building

✓ **Listen again, and fill in the blanks.**

W: Excuse me. Is there a restroom on this floor?

M: Yes, ma'am. It's ❶_____ the elevators.

W: Where are the elevators?

M: Walk straight ahead through the ❷_____
and turn left at the ❸_____ department.

W: Oh yes, I can see the toy ❹_____. Thank you.

M: You're welcome.

B

Dialog 2

Listen to the dialog and questions. Choose the best answer. ((Track 124))

1. (A) Buy a newspaper   (B) Eat dinner
   (C) Get some money   (D) Mail a letter

2. (A) It is not open.   (B) It is on Jefferson.
   (C) It is on the corner.   (D) It is very far away.

C

Dialog 3

Listen to the dialog, and write the missing information on the map. ((Track 125))

3. _____

They are here.   1. Highway _____

2. distance _____

5. distance _____

4. Highway _____

Hotel

Main Dialog

Listen to the dialog, and choose the best answer. ((Track 126))

1. Where are the speakers?
   - (A) In an airport
   - (B) In a hotel
   - (C) In a museum
   - (D) In a store

2. Where will the bus take the woman?
   - (A) To a hotel
   - (B) To a museum
   - (C) To a shopping mall
   - (D) To a subway station

3. How will she know the correct building?
   - (A) The building is pink.
   - (B) The driver will tell her.
   - (C) The roof is round.
   - (D) The walls are green.

Listen again, and fill in the blanks. ((Track 127))

W: Hi. I'd like to visit the art museum. Is it far from this hotel?

M: It's too far to walk, but you ❶_____ take the bus.

W: Where's the bus stop?

M: You will see a ❷_____ to your right, outside. You can take Bus ❸_____ there.

W: Does Bus 64 stop at the art ❹_____?

M: No, it stops at Union Street ❺_____ station. From there, you'll be able to see the museum one block down.

W: How will I ❻_____ it?

M: It's a pink ❼_____ building.

W: Great! Thanks for ❽_____ help.

Short Talks

Short Talk 1

Listen to the short talk and questions. Choose the best answer. (((Track 128)))

1. (A) Four blocks   (B) Four miles
   (C) Four streets   (D) Four kilometers

2. (A) Main Street   (B) Stop Light Street
   (C) University Drive   (D) Wright Lane

✓ **Listen again, and fill in the blanks.**

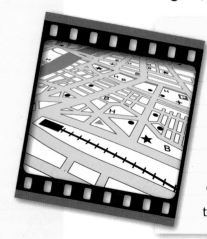

Take Highway 75 south from Hampton Parkway. Take the Greenville Avenue ❶_____ off the highway. At the first stop light after you exit, turn right. Drive for about four kilometers along Greenville. You will pass several ❷_____ while you are driving. At the stop light where Greenville meets ❸_____, turn right. This street will take you to the main ❹_____ of the university.

B

Short Talk 2

Listen to the short talk and questions. Choose the best answer. (((Track 129)))

1. (A) First   (B) Second
   (C) Third   (D) Fourth

2. (A) A door   (B) Another hallway
   (C) A sign   (D) Office numbers

C

Short Talk 3

Listen to the short talk, and circle the directions that the speaker gives. (((Track 130)))

across the street   drive there from here

look to your right   next to the café

the end of this street   turn left at the stop sign

Listening Quiz

04:15

A

Picture Matching

Listen to the dialogs. Choose the correct picture. ((Track 131))

 **A**

 **B**

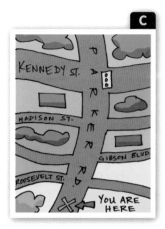 **C**

1. (A)   (B)   (C)

2. (A)   (B)   (C)

B

Listen & Choose

Listen to the dialogs and questions. Choose the best answer. ((Track 132))

3. (A) From a compass   (B) From the stars
   (C) From the sun   (D) From the south

4. (A) In another building   (B) Near the front door
   (C) On the next floor   (D) Outside the building

5. (A) A hotel   (B) A room
   (C) The pool   (D) The stairs

6. (A) In an airport   (B) In a hospital
   (C) In a school   (D) In a supermarket

7. (A) By the front door   (B) At the end of the aisle
   (C) On the bottom shelf   (D) Under the cash register

8. (A) Seats   (B) The box office
   (C) The exit   (D) The stage

9. (A) She is confused.   (B) She knows the way well.
   (C) She is hungry.   (D) She wants to go home.

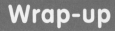

Wrap-up

A

Pre-listening Discussion

Talk about these questions.

1. Do you know which way is north right now?
2. Are you good at finding places and knowing directions?
3. If a man and a woman go on a driving trip, who usually drives? Why?

B

Listening Comprehension

Listen and answer the questions. ((Track 133))

1. **Who did the researcher study?**

   The researcher studied _____.

2. **Who usually did better at finding directions, men or women?**

   _____ did better at finding directions.

3. **What do some researchers say women are better at than men?**

   Some researchers say women are better at _____

   _____.

C

Dictation Practice

Listen again, and fill in the blanks. ((Track 134))

Many people believe that ❶_____ are better at ❷_____ directions than ❸_____. Maybe that is why ❹_____ usually drive when ❺_____ go somewhere. But is it ❻_____ true that men are ❼_____ at directions than ❽_____? Some researchers have ❾_____ to find out.

One ❿_____ studying this question ⓫_____ at men and women ⓬_____ were training to be ⓭_____. As part of their training, the ⓮_____ and women had to ⓯_____ their way through forests ⓰_____ over mountains. The researcher ⓱_____ an interesting difference between the ⓲_____ and women. Most of the ⓳_____ used the directions north, ⓴_____, east, and west along ㉑_____ big things around them, like ㉒_____ or the sun, to ㉓_____ their way. On the other ㉔_____, the women found their ㉕_____ by going from one ㉖_____ to the next without ㉗_____ their larger environment. In this ㉘_____, the men usually did ㉙_____ than the women.

Other ㉚_____ have studied how men's ㉛_____ women's brains work. Some ㉜_____ that men are better at ㉝_____ puzzles and imagining objects. ㉞_____ are better at using ㉟_____ and communicating.

PART I: Picture Description (Track 135)

Listen and choose the statement that best describes what you see in the picture.

1.

    (A)   (B)   (C)   (D)

2.

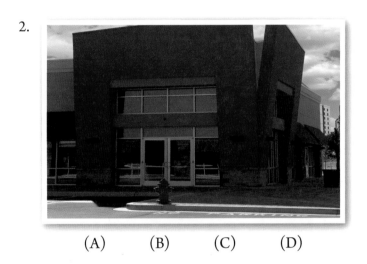

    (A)   (B)   (C)   (D)

3.

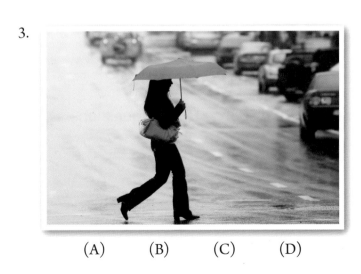

    (A)   (B)   (C)   (D)

4.

(A)   (B)   (C)   (D)

5.

(A)   (B)   (C)   (D)

PART II: Questions and Responses ((Track 136))

Listen and choose the best response to each question.

6. (A)   (B)   (C)

7. (A)   (B)   (C)

8. (A)   (B)   (C)

9. (A)   (B)   (C)

10. (A)   (B)   (C)

PART III: Short Conversations ((Track 137))

You will hear two dialogs, each followed by three questions. Listen carefully, and choose the best answer to each question.

11. Which direction should the woman go?

   (A) North
   (B) East
   (C) Northeast
   (D) The man does not know

12. Where are the speakers?

   (A) In a shuttle
   (B) In a hotel
   (C) At the gym
   (D) In a car

13. What does the man recommend that the woman do?

   (A) Take a taxi
   (B) Take the shuttle
   (C) Wait in the lobby
   (D) Go to the History Museum

---

14. Which is true about the woman?

   (A) She does not like her dentist.
   (B) She has a dental appointment.
   (C) She is the man's dentist.
   (D) She works downtown.

15. What does the man offer?

   (A) To call the office
   (B) To take her to the dentist
   (C) To give the office her number
   (D) To drive her downtown

16. What street is the office located?

   (A) Bellview
   (B) Fourth Street
   (C) Downtown
   (D) Building Street

PART IV: Short Talks ((Track 138))

You will hear two talks, each followed by three questions. Listen carefully, and choose the best answer to each question.

17. How should a person travel to this location?

    (A) By bus
    (B) By subway
    (C) By taxi
    (D) By car

18. What do the instructions say NOT to do?

    (A) Enter the mall
    (B) Go up to the street
    (C) Look for signs
    (D) Take the green line

19. Why do the instructions state that it should be easy to find?

    (A) There are guides available to help.
    (B) There are signs in the subway station.
    (C) There is a mall connection.
    (D) There are two lines that go to the same place.

---

20. How does a person get to the third floor?

    (A) Take the stairs
    (B) Take an escalator
    (C) Through the glass doors
    (D) Take the elevator

21. Where can a person get information on equipment in the spa?

    (A) At the hotel lobby's main desk
    (B) By calling a special number
    (C) At the spa's reception desk
    (D) From any hotel employee

22. How can a person recognize the spa entrance?

    (A) It has glass doors.
    (B) The door is very small.
    (C) The hallway is long and wide.
    (D) There is a desk in front of it.

UNIT 7

School

Warm-up

A
Look & Listen

Listen to the dialogs. ((Track 139))

B
Listen Again

Listen again, and circle the correct word or phrase. ((Track 140))

1. Jason (did / didn't do) his homework.
2. Billy (can / can't) play soccer in the afternoon.
3. Jenny (has / doesn't have) her pencil case.
4. Anne (was / wasn't) sick yesterday.

C
Essential Expressions

Who would probably say each statement or question?
Check (✓) the correct person.   Teachers   Students

1. Please pass your homework to the front.
2. Can I borrow your notes?
3. This is my sophomore year.
4. Let me see if I have an extra pen in my backpack.
5. I'd like to remind all of you about the exam on Friday.
6. Our study group meets in the library Wednesday after school.
7. I feel sick. May I go see the school nurse?
8. I'm not really involved in any extracurricular activities.
9. Work in pairs. Check your answers together.
10. That's all for today, but don't forget to turn in your
    assignments before you leave class.

Listening Practice

Listen. Write the answer. ((Track 141))

About twenty-five.	Choir.	Mr. Oliver.
No, it wasn't.	Yes, I think it's fun.	

1. _____
2. _____
3. _____
4. _____
5. _____

Listen. Write the question. ((Track 142))

What did you get on the exam?	Do you like this class?	When is the test?
What is your teacher's name?	How long is the class?	

1. _____
2. _____
3. _____
4. _____
5. _____

Describe the picture using the words below.

graduate	diploma	pose	gown

✓ **Listen to the description of the picture.** ((Track 143))

A

Intonation Practice

In certain two-syllable statements or questions, the stress will usually be on the second syllable. Study these statements and questions that have the last syllable stressed.

Written	Spoken
1. What time?	1. What **time**?
2. Hello?	2. Hel**lo**?
3. It's me.	3. It's **me**.

✓ **Now practice saying the following sentences. Remember to stress the second syllable.**

1. Really?
2. That's right.
3. What's up?

✓ **Now listen and repeat.** ((Track 144))

B

Conversation Pictures

Listen to the dialogs, and number the pictures. ((Track 145))

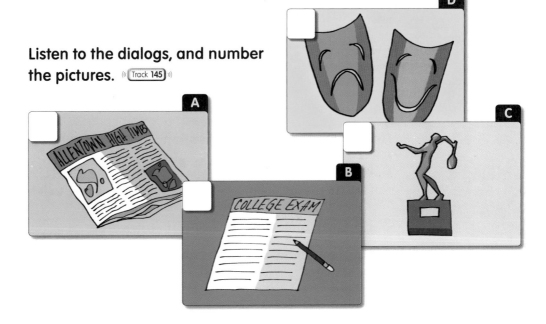

✓ **Now listen to the dialogs again, and match the year in school with the activity.**

1. freshman •
2. sophomore •
3. junior •
4. senior •

• (A) acting
• (B) sports
• (C) studying
• (D) writing

Short Dialogs

A
Dialog 1

Listen to the dialog and questions. Choose the best answer. ((Track 146))

1. (A) He already ate lunch.   (B) He did not do the homework.
   (C) He is good at math.   (D) He wants to help the woman.

2. (A) The man can't finish it quickly.   (B) The man does not like math.
   (C) The man is a good student.   (D) The man will get a good score.

✓ **Listen again, and fill in the blanks.**

W: Did you finish the math homework yet?

M: No, I haven't even ❶_____ it.

W: Too bad. I thought we could check our
   ❷_____ together.

M: I was planning to do the homework during
   lunch. Maybe we can check it then.

W: There is ❸_____ you can finish all
   those problems during ❹_____.

M: I can if you help me.

B
Dialog 2

Listen to the dialog and questions. Choose the best answer. ((Track 147))

1. (A) Home   (B) To see his teacher
   (C) To the nurse   (D) To the toilet

2. (A) He is lazy.   (B) He is lying.
   (C) He likes the nurse. (D) He is ill.

C
Dialog 3

Listen to the dialog, and complete each statement. ((Track 148))

1. The exam is on _____.

2. She has reviewed her notes up to _____.

Main Dialog

Listen

A. Listen to the dialog, and choose the best answer. (Track 149)

1. Why does he think she is a high school student?
   - (A) Her age
   - (B) Her backpack
   - (C) Her books
   - (D) Her clothes

2. What year of high school is she in?
   - (A) First
   - (B) Second
   - (C) Third
   - (D) Fourth

3. Which class is she probably taking?
   - (A) Biology
   - (B) French
   - (C) Geometry
   - (D) Literature

Listen Again

B. Listen again, and fill in the blanks. (Track 150)

B: Hi. My name is Tim.

G: Hi, Tim. I'm Martha.

B: I noticed your school ❶_____.
What school do you go to?

G: I go to Longfellow High School.
❷_____ about you?

B: I go to Central High. What ❸_____
are you in?

G: I'm a ❹_____.

B: Me, too! If we went to the ❺_____ school,
we would probably be in lots
of the same ❻_____.

G: Maybe. At Longfellow we get to ❼_____
classes to fit our interests, so I'm taking some
extra science classes. Do you like those kinds of
subjects?

B: Uh, not really. I'm more into
❽_____ and English.

Short Talks

A

Short Talk 1

Listen to the short talk and questions. Choose the best answer. ((Track 151))

1. (A) Students who like art   (B) Students who like math
   (C) Students who like sports   (D) Students who like writing

2. (A) A book   (B) A play
   (C) A presentation   (D) A sport's competition

✓ **Listen again, and fill in the blanks.**

I am glad to see that so many ❶_____ at our school are interested in starting a writing club. Since this is our club's first meeting, we need to decide how our ❷_____ should be organized. I hope we can all share the ❸_____ that we write during this school year. One of our teachers, Mr. Greenwald, has ❹_____ to help our club put together a small book at the end of the year.

B

Short Talk 2

Listen to the short talk and questions. Choose the best answer. ((Track 152))

1. (A) A salesperson   (B) A secretary
   (C) A student   (D) A teacher

2. (A) She did not go to class.   (B) She did not study at home.
   (C) She did not take tests.   (D) She did not write an essay.

C

Short Talk 3

Listen to the short talk, and complete the note diagram. ((Track 153))

Ancient _____ Techniques

Speaker: _____	_____ : Rome	Julia: _____
• techniques	• _____	• _____
• _____	• crops	• _____

Listening Quiz

A

Picture Matching

Listen to the dialogs. Choose the correct picture. (((Track 154)))

 A
 B
 C

1. (A)   (B)   (C)

2. (A)   (B)   (C)

B

Listen & Choose

Listen to the dialogs and questions. Choose the best answer. (((Track 155)))

3. (A) After school   (B) Before lunch
   (C) During break time   (D) In class

4. (A) A classmate   (B) Homework problems
   (C) Studying together   (D) Test results

5. (A) It is boring.   (B) It is difficult.
   (C) It is good.   (D) It is finished.

6. (A) He doesn't have time.   (B) He doesn't know.
   (C) He doesn't like sports. (D) He doesn't play well.

7. (A) They are easy.   (B) They are getting worse.
   (C) They are improving.   (D) They are the same.

8. (A) Go to a museum   (B) Go to England
   (C) Go to a theater   (D) Go to the zoo

9. (A) Read it   (B) Saw it
   (C) Took it   (D) Wrote it

Wrap-up

A

Pre-listening Discussion

Talk about these questions.

1. What time do schools end each day in your country?
2. Do many students spend time at school after classes finish? What do they do?
3. Who usually watches young children if both parents work?

B

Listening Comprehension

Listen and answer the questions. ((Track 156))

1. **Why do students usually go to after-school programs in elementary school?**
   Students usually go to after-school programs in elementary school because
   _____.

2. **How are some after-school programs better than day care programs?**
   Some after-school programs are better than day care programs because _____
   _____.

3. **What are three things children may do in an after-school program?**
   Three things children may do in an after-school program are _____,
   _____, and _____.

C

Dictation Practice

Listen again, and fill in the blanks. ((Track 157))

Many high school ❶_____ in the United States take ❷_____ in school activities such as ❸_____, choirs, bands, math clubs, ❹_____ clubs, and theater activities. But after-school ❺_____ are not just for high school ❻_____. Many elementary schools also have after-school ❼_____ for students.

Most of the students in ❽_____ after-school programs cannot go ❾_____ when school ends because both ❿_____ work. These students are too ⓫_____ to stay at home alone. So the ⓬_____ purpose of these programs is ⓭_____ to watch the children until their ⓮_____ can take them home. The ⓯_____ part is that many of the ⓰_____ in elementary schools are ⓱_____ for parents, unlike professional daycare ⓲_____ that are usually very ⓳_____.

The teachers in charge of the ⓴_____ want the children to learn ㉑_____ they are there. So the ㉒_____ may have a special time for ㉓_____ to do their homework. Many ㉔_____ also keep the school library ㉕_____ for students. Students can go to the ㉖_____ to read books or to use the library's ㉗_____. But after-school programs are not "㉘_____ work." There is also plenty of ㉙_____ for children to play on the school's ㉚_____.

Listening Test

PART I: Picture Description ((Track 158))

Listen and choose the statement that best describes what you see in the picture.

1.

    (A)   (B)   (C)   (D)

2.

    (A)   (B)   (C)   (D)

3.

    (A)   (B)   (C)   (D)

4.

(A)   (B)   (C)   (D)

5.

(A)   (B)   (C)   (D)

PART II: Questions and Responses ((Track 159))

Listen and choose the best response to each question.

6. (A)   (B)   (C)

7. (A)   (B)   (C)

8. (A)   (B)   (C)

9. (A)   (B)   (C)

10. (A)   (B)   (C)

PART III: Short Conversations ((Track 160))

You will hear two dialogs, each followed by three questions. Listen carefully, and choose the best answer to each question.

11. What does the man remind everyone of?

    (A) The exam will be next week.
    (B) He will be late for the exam.
    (C) Lunch will be next week.
    (D) The review session is coming soon.

12. What problem does the woman have?

    (A) She doesn't want to review for the exam.
    (B) She wants to review on a different day.
    (C) She has plans on the day of the review session.
    (D) She isn't ready to take the exam.

13. What was the main subject of the conversation?

    (A) How to study for the exam
    (B) Scheduling the family lunch
    (C) Scheduling the exam review
    (D) Difficulty of the exam

---

14. What did the man say he wanted?

    (A) To leave
    (B) To delay the test for one more week
    (C) To cancel the test
    (D) To have more test reviews

15. What was the woman's response to the man's request?

    (A) She said no.
    (B) She said she would think about it.
    (C) She told him to study a lot more.
    (D) She did not respond.

16. What does the man wish?

    (A) That he had studied more
    (B) That he had attended every class
    (C) That the teacher would listen to him
    (D) That he had more time to review

PART IV: Short Talks ((Track 161))

You will hear two talks, each followed by three questions. Listen carefully, and choose the best answer to each question.

17. Where does this teacher probably work?

(A) At an elementary school
(B) At a high school
(C) At a university
(D) At a community college

18. What did this teacher say about his work?

(A) He gets up early to go to work.
(B) He thinks the children are rude.
(C) He sometimes doesn't feel like he's working.
(D) He thinks it can be very relaxing.

19. How difficult does he think his job is?

(A) It is hard work.
(B) It is easy work.
(C) It is sometimes difficult.
(D) It is not difficult at all.

---

20. What does the speaker do?

(A) She is a teacher.
(B) She is a writer.
(C) She is a student.
(D) She is a librarian.

21. When does the speaker go to her music class?

(A) In her first class
(B) Before lunch
(C) Right after lunch
(D) After school

22. What does she like about her classes?

(A) The books
(B) The classmates
(C) The homework
(D) The teachers

UNIT 8 Sports

Warm-up

Listen to the dialogs. ((Track 162))

Listen again, and fill in the blanks. ((Track 163))

1. He lets Sally use his _____.
2. Lisa wants to kick the ball _____.
3. Both men know how to make the Frisbee _____.
4. Kate started skateboarding when she was _____.

Write the missing words to make correct expressions.

bowl	coach	competitive	defense	field
playing	points	throw	tickets	volleyball

1. Before she became a _____, she was a famous player in the sport.
2. It's hard to stay _____ in the game when you're tired.
3. There are nine players on the _____ right now.
4. Do you want to go _____ the ball around?
5. Our team is better at offense than at _____.
6. He scored three _____ in the last game.
7. Do you know how to play _____?
8. I can't afford to buy season _____.
9. Have you been _____ for a long time?
10. Would you rather _____ or play pool?

Listening Practice

A
How would you answer?

Listen. Write the answer. (((Track 164)))

My friend.	No, there isn't.	On the school field.
Twice a week.	Yes, I do.	

1. _____
2. _____
3. _____
4. _____
5. _____

B
How would you ask?

Listen. Write the question. (((Track 165)))

Have you played squash before?	Is water skiing fun?	Who did you play with?
Where do you exercise?	How often do you play basketball?	

1. _____
2. _____
3. _____
4. _____
5. _____

C
Picture Description

Describe the picture using the words below.

hold	ground	tackle	uniform

✓ **Listen to the description of the picture.** (((Track 166)))

Speaking Practice

In casual speech, you may hear the word "did" pronounced as "d" after *wh*-words.

Written	Spoken
1. What did he do last night?	1. What'd he do last night?
2. Why did they stop playing?	2. Why'd they stop playing?
3. Who did she go swimming with?	3. Who'd she go swimming with?

✓ **Now practice saying the following sentences.**

1. When did she learn to play?
2. Where did my friend go?
3. Why did they choose that player?

✓ **Now listen and repeat.** ((Track 167))

B
Conversation Pictures

Listen to the dialogs, and number the pictures. ((Track 168))

✓ **Now listen to the dialogs again, and choose the correct topic of the conversation.**

1. (A) A player   (B) Food   (C) The coach   (D) The seats
2. (A) A player   (B) Food   (C) The coach   (D) The seats
3. (A) A player   (B) Food   (C) The coach   (D) The seats
4. (A) A player   (B) Food   (C) The coach   (D) The seats

Short Dialogs

A

Dialog 1

Listen to the dialog and questions. Choose the best answer. (((Track 169)))

1. (A) Daily
   (C) Every week
   (B) At least once a month
   (D) A few times a year

2. (A) His team
   (C) His partner
   (B) His equipment
   (D) His skill

✓ **Listen again, and fill in the blanks.**

W: How often do you play tennis?

M: Not as often as I'd like to. I only play once or twice a ❶_____.

W: Have you been ❷_____ tennis for a long time?

M: Since I was in high school. I was actually on my school's tennis ❸_____.

W: You must be pretty good, then.

M: I was better when I played regularly. Now I'm out of ❹_____.

B

Dialog 2

Listen to the dialog and questions. Choose the best answer. (((Track 170)))

1. (A) She's tired.
   (C) She hates bowling.
   (B) She wants to do something outdoors.
   (D) She has to take bowling lessons.

2. (A) He is afraid of animals.
   (C) He prefers bowling.
   (B) He thinks she's too old to visit the zoo.
   (D) He thinks it is too hot outside.

C

Dialog 3

Listen to the dialog, and check (✓) the information that can be inferred from what is said. (((Track 171)))

1. ☐ Their team has fewer points.   2. ☐ The woman likes player number 17.
   ☐ Their team has more points.   ☐ The woman doesn't like player number 17.

Listen to the dialog, and choose the best answer. (((Track 172)))

1. According to the woman, how will exercise benefit him?
   - (A) He will feel happier.
   - (B) It will help him study better.
   - (C) He will stay healthy.
   - (D) It will make him stronger.

2. What does the man think he needs in order to exercise?
   - (A) A coach
   - (B) A place to exercise
   - (C) An exercise partner
   - (D) Exercise equipment

3. What does the man suggest they play?
   - (A) A game
   - (B) A team sport
   - (C) A water sport
   - (D) A two-player sport

Listen again, and fill in the blanks. (((Track 173)))

W: Do you ❶_____ much?

M: Not really. I don't have time.

W: You should ❷_____ time. Exercise is good for your ❸_____.

M: I know, but I can't ❹_____ myself to do it.

W: Find a ❺_____ or some kind of exercise you enjoy. Then it will be easier.

M: I think the best thing is to find a friend to exercise with. Then working out won't be ❻_____.

W: Well, maybe we can work out by ❼_____ a sport together. What do you like to play?

M: I'm pretty good at ❽_____. Do you like to play that?

Short Talks

Listen to the short talk and questions. Choose the best answer. ((Track 174))

1. (A) Basketball   (B) Hockey
   (C) Soccer   (D) Volleyball

2. (A) It was a very close game.   (B) The other team had a lot more points.
   (C) Our team scored no points.   (D) The other team scored fewer points.

✓ **Listen again, and fill in the blanks.**

Our school's girls' ❶_____ team played their first game last Friday. Unfortunately, they lost the game. The final score was nine to three. The other team's offense and ❷_____ were both very strong. The ❸_____ player on our team was Nancy Taylor. She scored ❹_____. Michelle Robertson scored our team's third goal.

Listen to the short talk and questions. Choose the best answer. ((Track 175))

1. (A) They are nervous.   (B) They are proud.
   (C) They are strong.   (D) They are young.

2. (A) Equipment   (B) Speed
   (C) Techniques   (D) Understanding of the rules

Listen to the short talk, and number the events in order from 1-4. ((Track 176))

_____ (A) Competed in swimming competitions

_____ (B) Learned to dive

_____ (C) Started lessons with a coach

_____ (D) Was able to swim across the pool

Listening Quiz

Listen to the dialogs. Choose the correct picture. ((Track 177))

1. (A)   (B)   (C)

2. (A)   (B)   (C)

B

**Listen
& Choose**

Listen to the dialogs and questions. Choose the best answer. ((Track 178))

3. (A) Hitting the ball   (B) How the playing area looks
   (C) Scoring   (D) The equipment used

4. (A) Asking for help   (B) Coaching him
   (C) Scheduling a game   (D) Teaching him a rule

5. (A) None   (B) One
   (C) Two   (D) Three

6. (A) Nothing   (B) Two dollars
   (C) Six dollars   (D) Ten dollars

7. (A) Counting the score   (B) Looking for a place to play
   (C) Starting a game   (D) Taking a break

8. (A) Bring water for her   (B) Buy himself a drink
   (C) Fix the machine   (D) Take a shower

9. (A) Zero to zero   (B) One to one
   (C) Five to zero   (D) Five to five

Wrap-up

Talk about these questions.

1. Which sports do you like to watch on television?
2. What sport or activity do you do most often?
3. How often do you do this sport or activity?

A

Pre-listening Discussion

Listen and answer the questions. ((Track 179))

B

Listening Comprehension

1. **Which sports are popular on American television?**
   _____, _____, and _____ are popular on American television.

2. **Why isn't soccer shown on American television?**
   Soccer isn't shown on American television because _____
   _____.

3. **What is the most popular sport in America?**
   The most popular sport in America is _____.

Listen again, and fill in the blanks. ((Track 180))

C

Dictation Practice

There is a difference ❶_____ the most popular sport Americans ❷_____ and the most popular sport they ❸_____.

The most popular sports ❹_____ on television in the United States are ❺_____, basketball, and baseball. In other ❻_____ around the world, soccer is the ❼_____ popular sport on television, but ❽_____ is not usually shown on American ❾_____. This is probably because it is not ❿_____ for television channels to show ⓫_____ during soccer games. In football, ⓬_____, and baseball, there are many ⓭_____ during the game, and ⓮_____ can be shown in these ⓯_____. Although many Americans ⓰_____ football, basketball, and baseball in their ⓱_____ time, none of these sports ⓲_____ as the most popular sport in ⓳_____. The number of people watching ⓴_____ sports is much higher than the ㉑_____ playing these three sports. From a ㉒_____, sport researchers found that ㉓_____ was the most popular ㉔_____ in the United States.

Listening Test

PART I: Picture Description ((Track 181))

Listen and choose the statement that best describes what you see in the picture.

1.

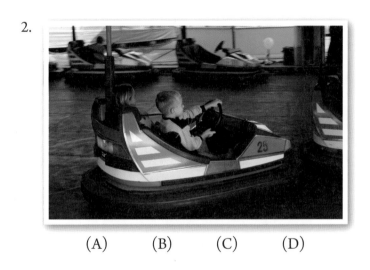

      (A)   (B)   (C)   (D)

2.

      (A)   (B)   (C)   (D)

3.

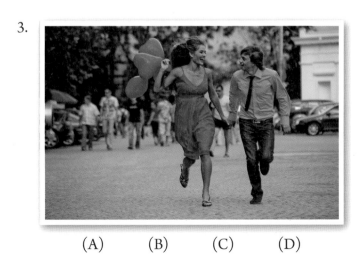

      (A)   (B)   (C)   (D)

4.

(A)   (B)   (C)   (D)

5.

(A)   (B)   (C)   (D)

PART II: Questions and Responses ((Track 182))

Listen and choose the best response to each question.

6. (A)   (B)   (C)

7. (A)   (B)   (C)

8. (A)   (B)   (C)

9. (A)   (B)   (C)

10. (A)   (B)   (C)

PART III: Short Conversations ((Track 183))

You will hear two dialogs, each followed by three questions. Listen carefully, and choose the best answer to each question.

11. What will the woman do?

    (A) Give the man medicine

    (B) Exercise with the man

    (C) Play another game

    (D) Stay home

12. What does the man invite the woman to do?

    (A) Have lunch

    (B) Jog around the park

    (C) Play some basketball

    (D) Relax

13. What does the woman think made her feel sick?

    (A) Talking with the man

    (B) Eating too much

    (C) Eating some potato salad

    (D) Sleeping too little

---

14. Which player does the man ask the woman to choose?

    (A) The best player in history

    (B) The player she likes the most

    (C) The best player these days

    (D) The first player to come to mind

15. What question does the woman think is silly?

    (A) What skill do you like best?

    (B) Do you like him for his skill or his personality?

    (C) What personality do you like the most?

    (D) How many languages did he speak?

16. What was the woman's last point in the conversation?

    (A) There are many good baseball players.

    (B) She appreciates skill more than personality.

    (C) The man shouldn't ask silly questions.

    (D) Baseball is a fun sport to watch.

PART IV: Short Talks (« Track 184 »)

You will hear two talks, each followed by three questions. Listen carefully, and choose the best answer to each question.

17. What sport is described in this information?

   (A) Baseball
   (B) Rock climbing
   (C) Tennis
   (D) Wrestling

18. What part of the sport is described?

   (A) Famous atheletes from this sport
   (B) How to keep score
   (C) Special actions before starting
   (D) How to play

19. Why do the athletes use salt?

   (A) To eat during rest periods
   (B) To make things dry
   (C) To purify things
   (D) To trick the other player

---

20. Who might benefit from this tip?

   (A) Very young players
   (B) Professional players
   (C) Older players
   (D) Female players

21. What does the tip explain?

   (A) How to choose good equipment
   (B) How to stay in shape
   (C) Why you should play with a partner
   (D) Strategies for scoring

22. What part of the body does the tip focus on?

   (A) The legs
   (B) The ankles
   (C) Biceps in the arms
   (D) Muscles in the upper body

UNIT 9 Appearance

Look & Listen

Warm-up

Listen to the dialogs. ((Track 185))

Listen Again

Listen again, and write the correct phrase to describe each person. ((Track 186))

had long hair for years	had dyed hair in the photo
shaved his mustache later	wore glasses in high school

1. The bride _____.
2. Stanley _____.
3. The groom _____.
4. Her father _____.

Essential Expressions

Write each word or phrase in the correct category.

bald	cotton	curly hair	silk	made of wood
slim	tight	athletic	younger	mustache and beard

To describe people

_____

_____

_____

_____

_____

To describe things

_____

_____

_____

_____

Listening Practice

A

How would you answer?

Listen. Write the answer. ((Track 187))

Blue jeans and a T-shirt.   No, she doesn't.   Brown.
Yes, he is.   He is a little taller than me.

1. _____

2. _____

3. _____

4. _____

5. _____

B

How would you ask?

Listen. Write the question. ((Track 188))

Does he have short hair?   How tall is she?   What does she look like?
How will I recognize him?   What color is his tie?

1. _____

2. _____

3. _____

4. _____

5. _____

C

Picture Description

Describe the picture using the words below.

| friends | playground | wear | put |

✓ **Listen to the description of the picture.** ((Track 189))

Speaking Practice

A

Pronunciation Practice

In casual speech, you may hear the word "and" pronounced as "n."

Written	Spoken
1. She has blond hair and blue eyes.	1. She has blond hair 'n blue eyes.
2. It is red, white, and blue.	2. It's red, white, 'n blue.
3. I wore glasses for years and years.	3. I wore glasses for years 'n years.

✓ **Now practice saying the following sentences.**

1. It has black and white stripes.
2. The earrings and necklace are made of gold.
3. The bag is small and black, and it has an orange zipper.

✓ **Now listen and repeat.** ((Track 190))

B

Conversation Pictures

Listen to the dialogs, and number the pictures. ((Track 191))

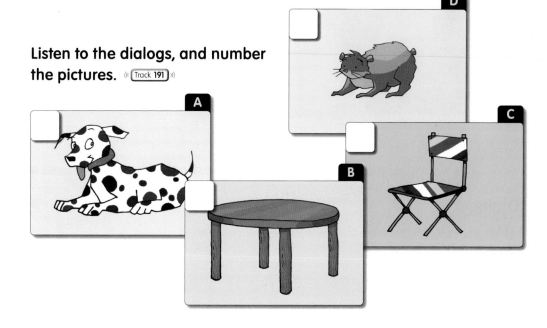

✓ **Now listen to the dialogs again, and choose the number of "yes" responses.**

1. (A) None   (B) One   (C) Two
2. (A) None   (B) One   (C) Two
3. (A) None   (B) One   (C) Two
4. (A) None   (B) One   (C) Two

Short Dialogs

A

Dialog 1

Listen to the dialog and questions. Choose the best answer. ((Track 192))

1. (A) Her brother   (B) Her father
   (C) Her husband   (D) Her uncle

2. (A) Huge   (B) Plump
   (C) Skinny   (D) Well-built

✓ **Listen again, and fill in the blanks.**

W: Excuse me. Have you seen an older man walking
around? I'm supposed to meet my father here, but I
haven't seen him.

M: What does he look like?

W: He has ❶_____ hair with a little gray in it.
He's about sixty years old.

M: Is he short and kind of ❷_____?

W: Yes, and he has a ❸_____.

M: I did see a man like that. He was sitting right over there
about ❹_____ minutes ago.

B

Dialog 2

Listen to the dialog and questions. Choose the best answer. ((Track 193))

1. (A) It was expensive.   (B) It was too big.
   (C) It was too small.   (D) It was ugly.

2. (A) A bracelet on her wrist   (B) A chain around her neck
   (C) Rings in her ears   (D) Rings on her fingers

C

Dialog 3

**Listen to the dialog, and circle the words or phrases that describe the
lamp.** ((Track 194))

| gold | green | metal | half a meter tall |

| silver | white | wood | one meter tall |

Main Dialog

Listen to the dialog, and choose the best answer. ((Track 195))

1. Why does the woman call the Lost and Found department?
   - (A) He called her.
   - (B) He found her wallet.
   - (C) She has his wallet.
   - (D) She is looking for something.

2. What does the woman NOT describe about the wallet?
   - (A) Its color
   - (B) Its material
   - (C) Its size
   - (D) Its texture

3. What will the man do?
   - (A) Buy her another wallet
   - (B) Call another location
   - (C) Mail her wallet to her
   - (D) Write down her name

Listen again, and fill in the blanks. ((Track 196))

M: Lost and Found. May I ❶_____ you?

W: Yes, I think I ❷_____ my wallet there this afternoon.

M: We've had a few wallets turned in. Can you ❸_____ the one you lost?

W: Yes, it is a black leather wallet.

M: Is the leather ❹_____ or does it have an alligator skin texture?

W: My wallet is smooth. And the clasp is ❺_____.

M: I'm sorry. There's no wallet here like the one you've ❻_____.

W: Could I ❼_____ my name and number in case it does show up there?

M: ❽_____, ma'am. What is your name?

Short Talks

A

Short Talk 1

Listen to the short talk and questions. Choose the best answer. ((Track 197))

1. (A) Buy furniture
   (C) Repair furniture

   (B) Paint furniture
   (D) Sell furniture

2. (A) It is antique.
   (C) It is damaged.

   (B) It is almost like new.
   (D) It is quite heavy.

✓ **Listen again, and fill in the blanks.**

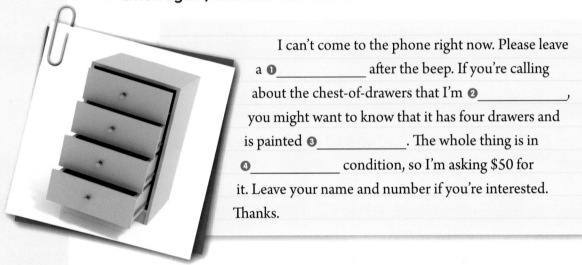

I can't come to the phone right now. Please leave a ❶_____ after the beep. If you're calling about the chest-of-drawers that I'm ❷_____, you might want to know that it has four drawers and is painted ❸_____. The whole thing is in ❹_____ condition, so I'm asking $50 for it. Leave your name and number if you're interested. Thanks.

B

Short Talk 2

Listen to the short talk and questions. Choose the best answer. ((Track 198))

1. (A) Animal doctors
   (C) People with pet snakes

   (B) Hikers in California
   (D) Zookeepers

2. (A) The eyes
   (C) The tail

   (B) The head
   (D) The teeth

C

Short Talk 3

Listen to the short talk, and complete each statement. ((Track 199))

1. The woman was carrying a _____.

2. She was wearing _____.

3. She also had on a _____.

Listening Quiz

04:29

A

Listen to the dialogs. Choose the correct picture. ((Track 200))

A

B

C

1. (A)   (B)   (C)

2. (A)   (B)   (C)

B

Listen to the dialogs and questions. Choose the best answer. ((Track 201))

3. (A) A high school girl
   (C) A middle-aged woman

   (B) A teenage boy
   (D) An old man

4. (A) A coat
   (C) A handbag

   (B) A dress
   (D) A suitcase

5. (A) Carmen was short.
   (C) The woman was fat.

   (B) Carmen was tall.
   (D) The woman was thin.

6. (A) He lost it.
   (C) It hurt him.

   (B) He sold it.
   (D) It is famous.

7. (A) It was dead.
   (C) It was big.

   (B) It was his dog.
   (D) It was someone's pet.

8. (A) Her eye color
   (C) Her height

   (B) Her hair color
   (D) Her weight

9. (A) Her age
   (C) Her height

   (B) Her job
   (D) Her interests

Wrap-up

A

Pre-listening Discussion

Talk about these questions.

1. What is your race?
2. What percent of the population in your country is this race?
3. Which race has the largest population in England?

B

Listening Comprehension

Listen and answer the questions. ((Track 202))

1. **What percent of the British population is white?**
   _____ of the British population is white.

2. **How are Newham and Brent different than other places in England?**
   Newham and Brent are different than other places in England because
   _____ .

3. **Which population is the largest minority in England?**
   The population that is the largest minority in England are _____ .

C

Dictation Practice

Listen again, and fill in the blanks. ((Track 203))

    Imagine a person from ❶_____ . Did you imagine a ❷_____ person? If you did, ❸_____ was a good picture of the ❹_____ person from England. In ❺_____ , most of the population of ❻_____ and Wales is white. ❼_____ you visit England, ❽_____ out of ten people you ❾_____ will be white.

    Although the ❿_____ of non-whites in England has ⓫_____ since World War II, there are ⓬_____ two places in England ⓭_____ minorities have become ⓮_____ . In Newham and Brent, ⓯_____ parts of London, races ⓰_____ than white make up more than ⓱_____ percent of the population in these ⓲_____ .

    According to the ⓳_____ census of England, ⓴_____ percent of the population is ㉑_____ . This includes whites from ㉒_____ , Europe, Australia, New Zealand, the ㉓_____ , and other countries. People from ㉔_____ make up the next largest ㉕_____ of people in England. ㉖_____ out of every 100 ㉗_____ in England are from ㉘_____ . Three out of every ㉙_____ people are from Pakistan. And ㉚_____ of every 400 people, ㉛_____ are from Bangladesh and ㉜_____ more are from China.

    ㉝_____ are a smaller minority than ㉞_____ in England. There are ㉟_____ equal numbers of blacks ㊱_____ Africa and the Caribbean. ㊲_____ two out of every ㊳_____ people are black: one ㊴_____ and one Caribbean.

Listening Test 🕐 08:40

PART I: Picture Description ((Track 204))

Listen and choose the statement that best describes what you see in the picture.

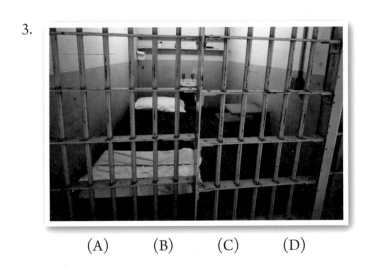

1.

(A)   (B)   (C)   (D)

2.

(A)   (B)   (C)   (D)

3.

(A)   (B)   (C)   (D)

4.

(A)   (B)   (C)   (D)

5.

(A)   (B)   (C)   (D)

PART II: Questions and Responses ((Track 205))

Listen and choose the best response to each question.

6. (A)   (B)   (C)

7. (A)   (B)   (C)

8. (A)   (B)   (C)

9. (A)   (B)   (C)

10. (A)   (B)   (C)

PART III: Short Conversations ((Track 206))

You will hear two dialogs, each followed by three questions. Listen carefully, and choose the best answer to each question.

11. Where are these people?
    - (A) At a restaurant
    - (B) At the airport
    - (C) In a clothing store
    - (D) In a museum

12. What did the woman offer?
    - (A) A larger size shirt
    - (B) A smaller size shirt
    - (C) An inexpensive shirt
    - (D) A more popular shirt

13. What did the man want the woman to do?
    - (A) He wanted her to go away.
    - (B) He wanted her to quickly get another shirt.
    - (C) He wanted her to find a different brand.
    - (D) He wanted her to take the shirt to the cash register.

---

14. What did the man first say about the woman?
    - (A) She should change her hair.
    - (B) She should say hello.
    - (C) He didn't recognize her immediately.
    - (D) He wanted her to look different.

15. What did the woman say she has been doing?
    - (A) She's been shopping more.
    - (B) She's been going to the barbershop.
    - (C) She's been on a diet.
    - (D) She's been going out more.

16. What did the woman do to her hair?
    - (A) She cut it shorter.
    - (B) She grew it longer.
    - (C) She made it curly.
    - (D) She dyed it a different color.

PART IV: Short Talks ((Track 207))

You will hear two talks, each followed by three questions. Listen carefully, and choose the best answer to each question.

17. What is being advertised?

(A) A book on child care
(B) A health club
(C) Children's clothing
(D) Sporting equipment

18. Which is NOT a feature of this product?

(A) It can change sizes.
(B) It is made for children.
(C) It is made of metal.
(D) It works well in winter.

19. Who is the advertisement directed toward?

(A) Children
(B) Coaches
(C) Parents
(D) Teachers

---

20. Which activity could this advice be applied to?

(A) Looking for a date
(B) Going to parties
(C) Studying at school
(D) Taking a photograph

21. What is the main idea of the tip?

(A) Take your time
(B) Tell the truth
(C) Think before you speak
(D) Work hard

22. What should you DO instead if you're worried about describing yourself?

(A) Not write a personal ad
(B) Describe only what you like about yourself
(C) Describe only your personality
(D) Describe only your looks

10

Weather

A
Look & Listen

Warm-up

Listen to the dialogs. ((Track 208))

B
Listen Again

Listen again, and fill in the blanks. ((Track 209))

Will take: _____   Won't take: _____

_____   _____

C
Essential
Expressions

Circle the correct phrase for each question.

1. How does it feel when there is a wonderful breeze?
   (A) Hot and humid   (B) Nice and cool

2. What happens when it is cloudy all day?
   (A) A hurricane will hit soon.   (B) The temperature stays down.

3. What might you expect when the temperature is below freezing?
   (A) Scattered showers   (B) Snow

4. How would you describe a day without a cloud in the sky?
   (A) Beautiful weather   (B) Quite a storm

5. What would you consider a high temperature?
   (A) About five degrees celsius   (B) Above 25 degrees celsius

Listening Practice

How would you answer?

Listen. Write the answer. ((Track 210))

No, I haven't.	I think so.	Not very cold.
Yes, you will.	No, it didn't.	

1. _____
2. _____
3. _____
4. _____
5. _____

B

How would you ask?

Listen. Write the question. ((Track 211))

Do you think it will rain?   How hot is it?   Will I need my umbrella?
Would you like to play tennis?   Didn't the weatherman say it would snow?

1. _____
2. _____
3. _____
4. _____
5. _____

C

Picture Description

Describe the picture using the words below.

cold	snow	build	mittens

✓ **Listen to the description of the picture.** ((Track 212))

Speaking Practice

A

Intonation Practice

In certain three-syllable statements or questions, the stress should be on the first and last syllables. Say these following statements and questions with the first and last syllable stressed.

Written	Spoken
1. We should go.	1. **We** should **go**.
2. Yes, it is.	2. **Yes**, it **is**.
3. Where is that?	3. **Where** is **that**?

✓ Now practice saying the following sentences. Remember to stress the first and last syllable.

1. I think so.
2. Is it cold?
3. What a day!

✓ Now listen and repeat. ((Track 213))

B

Conversation Pictures

Listen to the dialogs, and number the pictures. ((Track 214))

✓ Now listen to the dialogs again, and choose the correct location.

1. (A) Manaus   (B) Prudhoe Bay   (C) Oranjestad   (D) Tummu
2. (A) Manaus   (B) Prudhoe Bay   (C) Oranjestad   (D) Tummu
3. (A) Manaus   (B) Prudhoe Bay   (C) Oranjestad   (D) Tummu
4. (A) Manaus   (B) Prudhoe Bay   (C) Oranjestad   (D) Tummu

Short Dialogs

A
Dialog 1

Listen to the dialog and questions. Choose the best answer. ((Track 215))

1. (A) A large hat   (B) A raincoat
   (C) A summer dress   (D) A warm coat

2. (A) Clear skies   (B) Rain
   (C) Snow   (D) Fog

✓ **Listen again, and fill in the blanks.**

M: Did you finish packing for your business trip?

W: Not yet. I plan to finish packing tonight.

M: Make sure you take your heavy ❶_____.
I heard they're expecting a lot of snow in Chicago this weekend.

W: I hope it's not too bad. I'm supposed to fly back on ❷_____ afternoon.

M: Maybe things will ❸_____ up by then. I think most of the ❹_____ is expected on Friday and Saturday.

B
Dialog 2

Listen to the dialog and questions. Choose the best answer. ((Track 216))

1. (A) The same as always   (B) Hot and humid
   (C) Higher than usual   (D) Lower than usual

2. (A) A hat   (B) An umbrella
   (C) Sunglasses   (D) Sunscreen

C
Dialog 3

Listen to the dialog, and complete each statement. ((Track 217))

1. They both wrote down the _____ each day.

2. The first row of numbers shows the temperature in _____.

A

Listen

Listen to the dialog, and choose the best answer. ((Track 218))

1. What does the woman imply about the storm?
   (A) It was bright.   (B) It was dark.
   (C) It was loud.   (D) It was quiet.

2. Which is not mentioned as part of the storm?
   (A) Hail   (B) Lightning
   (C) Wind   (D) Rain

3. What can be inferred about the storm?
   (A) It was predicted early.   (B) It was typical for the season.
   (C) It was the worst in history.   (D) It was unusual for this time of year.

B

Listen Again

Listen again, and fill in the blanks. ((Track 219))

W: What a ❶_____ last night!

M: We had a ❷_____ storm last night? I didn't know that.

W: What? You mean the ❸_____ didn't wake you up?

M: No, I didn't hear a thing. It's too ❹_____, because I like thunderstorms.

W: You would have loved this one. There was ❺_____, lightning, wind, ❻_____ . . . .

M: How much rain fell?

W: I'm not exactly sure, but it must have been ❼_____ centimeters.

M: I hope I'm awake the next time a big storm blows through.

W: I bet you'll get to see one soon. This is the ❽_____ for storms like that.

Short Talks

Listen to the short talk and questions. Choose the best answer. ((Track 220))

1. (A) Having fun in the summer   (B) Avoiding skin problems
   (C) Growing plants   (D) Working outside in hot weather

2. (A) People get tired faster.   (B) People have darker skin.
   (C) People sweat more.   (D) People work more.

✓ **Listen again, and fill in the blanks.**

Now that it is August, we can expect hot and ❶_____
days for the next few weeks. I know a lot of people are going
to be working in their yards and gardens, but it is important
to remember to be ❷_____. Do yard work in the
morning or in the evening when the temperature is
❸_____. Also, drink lots of water because this
humid weather will make you ❹_____ more than
usual.

Listen to the short talk and questions. Choose the best answer. ((Track 221))

1. (A) In the east   (B) In the north
   (C) In the south   (D) In the west

2. (A) They don't have any snow.   (B) They have snow made by machines.
   (C) They have lots of snowmen.   (D) They will close for the weekend.

Listen to the short talk, and write T for true or F for false. ((Track 222))

1. _____ His grandmother has a lot of umbrellas.

2. _____ His grandmother does not go outside often because it rains too much.

3. _____ His grandmother sometimes uses an umbrella for shade.

Listening Quiz

04:38

Listen to the dialogs. Choose the correct picture. ((Track 223))

A

B

C

1. (A)   (B)   (C)

2. (A)   (B)   (C)

Listen to the dialogs and questions. Choose the best answer. ((Track 224))

3. (A) It is cold outside.   (B) It is raining.
    (C) The fog is lifting.   (D) The wind is blowing.

4. (A) March is cold.   (B) April is stormy.
    (C) May is warm.   (D) Spring is terrible.

5. (A) Cold   (B) Warm
    (C) Much hotter   (D) The same

6. (A) A big storm   (B) Heavy snow
    (C) Light rain   (D) Mild breezes

7. (A) A blackout   (B) A fire
    (C) A flood   (D) A tornado

8. (A) Cold and snowy   (B) Cool and windy
    (C) Hot and rainy   (D) Warm and dry

9. (A) It was frightening.   (B) It was great.
    (C) It was terrible.   (D) It was unusual.

Wrap-up

A
Pre-listening Discussion

Talk about these questions.

1. What is the best time of year to visit your country?
2. Does your country have a rainy season or a dry season? If yes, when?
3. What is the worst weather you have experienced in your hometown?

B
Listening Comprehension

Listen and answer the questions. ((Track 225))

1. **What weather condition produces high humidity for Hawaii?**
   High humidity in Hawaii is produced when _____
   _____ .

2. **What can you see in Hawaii if you visit during the rainy season?**
   If you visit Hawaii during the rainy season, you can see _____ .

3. **According to the reading, should people in Honolulu worry about hurricanes?**
   _____ , people in Honolulu _____ worry about hurricanes.

C
Dictation Practice

Listen again, and fill in the blanks. ((Track 226))

If you plan to ❶_____ to Hawaii, don't worry about the ❷_____ .
It is always "the best ❸_____ " to visit the islands.

❹_____ most of the year, there are ❺_____ blowing across
the Hawaiian ❻_____ . These are called the ocean "❼_____ " winds
because they ❽_____ trading ships travel to and ❾_____ the islands.
Sometimes during the ❿_____ , the usual trade winds ⓫_____ , and
the winds then ⓬_____ from the south. This is the most ⓭_____
time of year in ⓮_____ .

The rainy season for Hawaii ⓯_____ in November and ends
in ⓰_____ . But that does not ⓱_____ that it is a bad
⓲_____ of year to visit. On ⓳_____ days, it usually only
⓴_____ for a few hours, and then ㉑_____ can see
beautiful ㉒_____ .

The season for ㉓_____ around the Hawaiian Islands
㉔_____ from August through October. ㉕_____ in
Honolulu, where most people ㉖_____ , the hurricanes are rarely
㉗_____ . Most of the time, hurricanes only ㉘_____ stronger than
normal ㉙_____ .

PART I: Picture Description ((Track 227))

Listen and choose the statement that best describes what you see in the picture.

1.

    (A)   (B)   (C)   (D)

2.

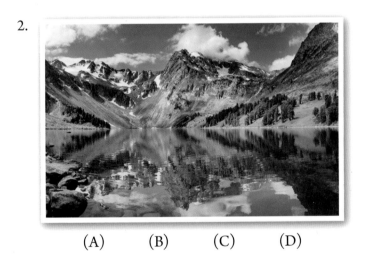

    (A)   (B)   (C)   (D)

3.

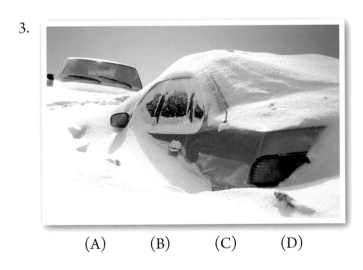

    (A)   (B)   (C)   (D)

4.

(A)   (B)   (C)   (D)

5.

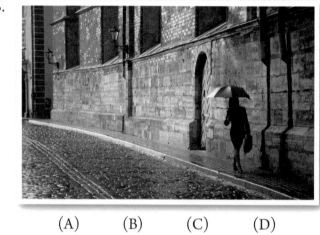

(A)   (B)   (C)   (D)

PART II: Questions and Responses ((Track 228))

Listen and choose the best response to each question.

6. (A)   (B)   (C)

7. (A)   (B)   (C)

8. (A)   (B)   (C)

9. (A)   (B)   (C)

10. (A)   (B)   (C)

PART III: Short Conversations (((Track 229)))

You will hear two dialogs, each followed by three questions. Listen carefully, and choose the best answer to each question.

11. What kind of weather does the woman expect?

    (A) Cold
    (B) Hot
    (C) Humid
    (D) Dry

12. Why did the man think it might rain?

    (A) He had been outside.
    (B) He read it in the newspaper.
    (C) The weather forecast said that it would be warmer.
    (D) It had been raining for days.

13. What did the woman think about the man's suggestion?

    (A) She disagreed with him.
    (B) She agreed with him.
    (C) She laughed.
    (D) She ignored him.

---

14. Which is true about the weather in this place in winter?

    (A) Hail often falls.
    (B) Ice never melts.
    (C) It is extremely wet.
    (D) It is very dry.

15. What was bothering the woman?

    (A) She didn't like the winter months.
    (B) She didn't like hand cream.
    (C) She had dry hands that hurt her.
    (D) She didn't want to go outside.

16. What made the weather nice in the summer, but worse in the winter?

    (A) The high humidity
    (B) The dry weather
    (C) The clear skies
    (D) The hot sun

PART IV: Short Talks ((Track 230))

You will hear two talks, each followed by three questions. Listen carefully, and choose the best answer to each question.

17. Which is true about the weather on Tuesday and Wednesday?
    (A) It will rain and hail.
    (B) It will rain continuously.
    (C) It will rain off and on.
    (D) It won't rain at all.

18. What is the prediction for Saturday's weather?
    (A) Cloudy skies
    (B) Rain
    (C) Strong winds
    (D) Lots of sunshine

19. Which day did the forecast say would be the best day for golf?
    (A) Tuesday
    (B) Wednesday
    (C) Thursday
    (D) Friday

___

20. What does this advice refer to?
    (A) Choosing clothing
    (B) Predicting the weather
    (C) Preparing for a storm
    (D) Protecting your skin

21. Which item is NOT suggested for use?
    (A) A long-sleeved shirt
    (B) Shorts
    (C) Sunglasses
    (D) Sunblock

22. When should a person put on sunblock?
    (A) Thirty minutes before going outside
    (B) Right after going outdoors
    (C) Thirty minutes after going out
    (D) At two o'clock in the afternoon

UNIT 11 Instructions

Warm-up

A
Look & Listen

Listen to the dialogs. ((Track 231))

B
Listen Again

Listen again, and number the steps in order from 1-4. ((Track 232))

_____ (A) Attach the sticker to the bag.
_____ (B) Look at the number.
_____ (C) Press enter.
_____ (D) Put the item or items on the scale.

C
Essential Expressions

Is the question or statement related to using a machine or writing something? Check (✓) the correct one.

	Using a machine	Writing something
1. When should I plug it in?	☐	☐
2. Can you help me fill out this order form?	☐	☐
3. First, you need to complete an application.	☐	☐
4. I'll just need some information from you.	☐	☐
5. Just wait a few seconds for it to warm up.	☐	☐
6. Please RSVP by June 15th.	☐	☐
7. From the menu on the screen, select open.	☐	☐
8. How do you make the player move?	☐	☐
9. Put in the number and press enter.	☐	☐
10. What do I need to say in the first sentence?	☐	☐

A

How would you answer?

Listen. Write the answer. ((Track 233))

No, I didn't.	First, turn it on.	Like this.
No, it's not.	Sure. What do you need?	

1. _____
2. _____
3. _____
4. _____
5. _____

B

How would you ask?

Listen. Write the question. ((Track 234))

Are we finished?	Is this right?	Where are they?
Can we do this by ourselves?		Have you done this before?

1. _____
2. _____
3. _____
4. _____
5. _____

C

Picture Description

Describe the picture using the words below.

plans	build	stairs	floor

✓ **Listen to the description of the picture.** ((Track 235))

A

Pronunciation Practice

In casual speech, you may hear the words "don't know" pronounced as "dunno."

Written	Spoken
1. I don't know how to use the machine.	1. I dunno how to use the machine.
2. We don't know where the switch is.	2. We dunno where the switch is.
3. People don't know how easy it is.	3. People dunno how easy it is.

✓ **Now practice saying the following sentences.**

1. I don't know how to do this.
2. What do I do if I don't know how to play the game?
3. They don't know how to complete the application.

✓ **Now listen and repeat.** ((Track 236))

B

Conversation Pictures

Listen to the dialogs, and number the pictures. ((Track 237))

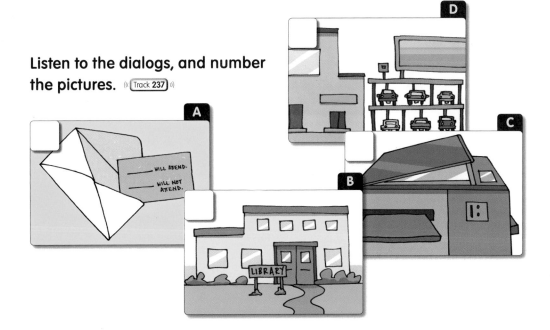

✓ **Now listen to the dialogs again, and choose the correct length of time.**

1. (A) Now (B) Less than one minute (C) Many hours (D) Next week
2. (A) Now (B) Less than one minute (C) Many hours (D) Next week
3. (A) Now (B) Less than one minute (C) Many hours (D) Next week
4. (A) Now (B) Less than one minute (C) Many hours (D) Next week

Short Dialogs

Listen to the dialog and questions. Choose the best answer. ((Track 238))

1. (A) Her card is not good.　　(B) She can't read the machine.
   (C) The machine is broken.　　(D) She lost all of her money.

2. (A) A PIN number　　(B) Cash
   (C) The amount she wants　　(D) Her card

✓ **Listen again, and fill in the blanks.**

W: Oh, no! All of the words on this ATM machine's screen are in Chinese.

M: I can help you. I ❶_____ a little Chinese.

W: I already put my card into the machine. What do I do now?

M: If you want to take money out, press the ❷_____ button over here. Then put in the ❸_____ you want.

W: Now what?

M: Now it's asking for your ❹_____.

W: Oh. It worked! Thanks a lot for your help.

Listen to the dialog and questions. Choose the best answer. ((Track 239))

1. (A) By playing all the cards　　(B) By playing any card
   (C) By playing the bottom card　　(D) By playing the top card

2. (A) Play another two cards　　(B) Put in more money
   (C) Stop the game　　(D) Take the cards back

Listen to the dialog and questions. Complete the answers. ((Track 240))

1. She is filling out _____.

2. He told her to list _____.

3. The woman won't _____.

Main Dialog

A
Listen

Listen to the dialog, and choose the best answer. (((Track 241)))

1. What are these instructions for?
   - (A) Buying flowers
   - (B) Drying flowers
   - (C) Growing flowers
   - (D) Naming flowers

2. What should the woman remove from the roses?
   - (A) Bugs
   - (B) Flowers
   - (C) Leaves
   - (D) Roots

3. How long will this process take?
   - (A) Several days
   - (B) A few weeks
   - (C) More than a month
   - (D) She does not say.

B
Listen Again

Listen again, and fill in the blanks. (((Track 242)))

W₁: That is a beautiful flower arrangement!

W₂: Thanks. I ❶_____ these roses myself.

W₁: Was it difficult?

W₂: No. ❷_____ flowers is really easy. You can try it yourself.

W₁: What do I ❸_____ to do first?

W₂: Take off all of the ❹_____ and thorns. Then cut the ❺_____ so they are 30 or 40 centimeters long. Take six or seven roses and ❻_____ the stems together about 5 centimeters from the bottom. Then hang them ❼_____ down so they can dry completely.

W₁: How long does that take?

W₂: Two or three ❽_____ should be long enough.

Short Talks

Listen to the short talk and questions. Choose the best answer. (Track 243)

1. (A) Hiking at night   (B) Leaving trash along the trail
   (C) Walking too far   (D) Putting too much water into a container

2. (A) Several days before hiking   (B) One day before hiking
   (C) The day of the hike   (D) The tip does not say.

✓ **Listen again, and fill in the blanks.**

When you go hiking this summer, carry a bottle of
❶_____ with you instead of a bottle of water. Take
any small plastic bottle and fill it ❷_____ full of
water. Don't completely fill the bottle, or it will break
when it ❸_____. Put the bottle in the freezer
❹_____ before you go hiking. While you are
hiking, the ice will melt, and you can enjoy a cool drink
anytime during the day.

Listen to the short talk and questions. Choose the best answer. (Track 244)

1. (A) An account name   (B) A credit card number
   (C) A salesperson's name   (D) An order number

2. (A) Buying software   (B) Downloading software
   (C) Previewing software   (D) Updating software

Listen to the short talk, and list two things that both sections should do. (Track 245)

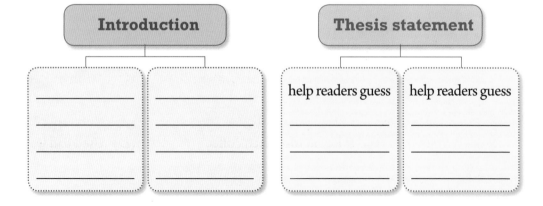

Introduction		Thesis statement	
_____	_____	help readers guess	help readers guess
_____	_____	_____	_____
_____	_____	_____	_____
_____	_____	_____	_____

A

Picture Matching

Listen to the dialogs. Choose the correct picture. ((Track 246))

A

B

C

1. (A)   (B)   (C)

2. (A)   (B)   (C)

B

Listen & Choose

Listen to the dialogs and questions. Choose the best answer. ((Track 247))

3. (A) They will come back later.   (B) They will hear the number.
   (C) They will see the number.   (D) They will wait in line.

4. (A) BBQ Beef   (B) Chicken Soup
   (C) Grilled Steak   (D) Italian Chicken

5. (A) Finding radio channels   (B) Installing a program
   (C) Playing a CD   (D) Using a VCR

6. (A) Check his passport   (B) Find her lost passport
   (C) Get a passport   (D) Replace a passport

7. (A) A form   (B) Her old passport
   (C) Identification   (D) Money

8. (A) Tried a new kind of coffee   (B) Drank too much coffee
   (C) Fixed the coffee machine   (D) Made bad coffee

9. (A) Broke the machine   (B) Not wait long enough
   (C) Put in too much coffee   (D) Used bad water

Pre-listening Discussion

A

Talk about these questions.

1. Are you good or bad at remembering the names of new people?
2. Do you have any tricks for remembering names? If yes, what are they?
3. Can these tricks be used to remember other things?

B

Listening Comprehension

Listen and answer the questions. (Track 248)

1. **What is the "best" way to remember someone's name?**
   _____.

2. **What are two things names can be connected with?**
   _____.

3. **What does the speaker suggest if you forget someone's name?**
   _____.

C

Dictation Practice

Listen again, and fill in the blanks. (Track 249)

Do you ever ❶_____ trouble remembering people's ❷_____? If you do, here are some ❸_____ you can use to help you ❹_____ the names of people you ❺_____.

The best way to remember ❻_____'s name is to repeat the ❼_____ over and over. You can ❽_____ the person's name while you ❾_____ to them. Or, if you have a ❿_____ or two while he or she is ⓫_____ talking to you, you can ⓬_____ the name in your ⓭_____. Repeating names in your ⓮_____ is a good way to remember ⓯_____ than one name if you meet ⓰_____ new people at the same time.

⓱_____ trick you can use to remember ⓲_____ is to connect the person's name to ⓳_____ else. If your friend Tom ⓴_____ you to Mike, you can ㉑_____ them together as "Tom ㉒_____ Mike." Or you can ㉓_____ the person's name to something ㉔_____ the person. If Sarah was ㉕_____ a silk shirt when you ㉖_____ her, it might help to remember ㉗_____ name as "Silk ㉘_____ Sarah."

In case you ㉙_____ someone's name, don't feel ㉚_____ about asking them to ㉛_____ it to you again. ㉜_____ forgets names now and ㉝_____. After hearing it ㉞_____, you'll probably remember it more ㉟_____ next time.

PART I: Picture Description ((Track 250))

Listen and choose the statement that best describes what you see in the picture.

1.

(A)   (B)   (C)   (D)

2.

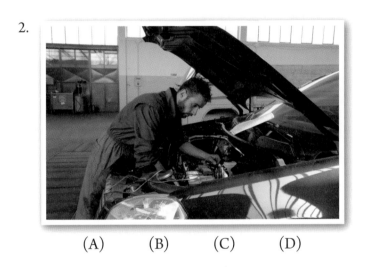

(A)   (B)   (C)   (D)

3.

(A)   (B)   (C)   (D)

4.

(A)　　(B)　　(C)　　(D)

5.

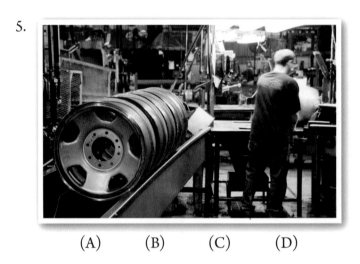

(A)　　(B)　　(C)　　(D)

PART II: Questions and Responses ((Track 251))

Listen and choose the best response to each question.

6. (A)　　(B)　　(C)

7. (A)　　(B)　　(C)

8. (A)　　(B)　　(C)

9. (A)　　(B)　　(C)

10. (A)　　(B)　　(C)

PART III: Short Conversations ((Track 252))

You will hear two dialogs, each followed by three questions. Listen carefully, and choose the best answer to each question.

11. Which is true about the fee?

    (A) She didn't want to pay it.

    (B) Her friend will pay it later.

    (C) It's higher than before.

    (D) She can't use a credit card.

12. What did the man first ask the woman to do?

    (A) Fill out a form

    (B) Pay the fee

    (C) Take the application to the counter

    (D) Go to an ATM machine

13. What does the woman plan to do?

    (A) Complete the application later

    (B) Withdraw some money at an ATM

    (C) Cash a check to pay the fee

    (D) Return to her home

---

14. What does the woman tell the man to do?

    (A) Hang the clothes on the line

    (B) Put all the clothes together

    (C) Separate the whites and colors

    (D) Use warm water

15. What did the man say about the water temperature?

    (A) Cold water is the best for washing different clothes.

    (B) Hot water cleans better than cold water.

    (C) It is best to clean clothes with warm water.

    (D) Cold water is less expensive to use.

16. What does the man want?

    (A) He wants everything to smell clean.

    (B) He wants to use a new type of detergent.

    (C) He wants to remove some stains.

    (D) He wants the woman to wash his clothes.

PART IV: Short Talks ((Track 253))

You will hear two talks, each followed by three questions. Listen carefully, and choose the best answer to each question.

17. What kind of advice is given?

    (A) How to act at parties
    (B) How to make friends
    (C) How to raise children
    (D) How to train pets

18. Which should you do when you feel angry?

    (A) Ignore the problem
    (B) Play a game
    (C) Share your feelings
    (D) Wait and calm down

19. When should you NOT ignore bad behavior?

    (A) If a child could get hurt
    (B) If other people complain
    (C) If someone sees you
    (D) If you are embarrassed

---

20. Who might need to use this tip?

    (A) Someone choosing a career
    (B) Someone fixing a house
    (C) Someone looking for an apartment
    (D) Someone working in an office

21. What is the benefit of following this tip?

    (A) A safer home
    (B) Better quality results
    (C) Good friends
    (D) More money

22. What is the main message of this tip?

    (A) Don't paint a house by yourself.
    (B) Always ask a professional to do the job.
    (C) Amateur work is never good.
    (D) Use wide tape to cover selected areas before you paint.

12 Stories

Warm-up

A
Look & Listen

Listen to the dialogs. (((Track 254)))

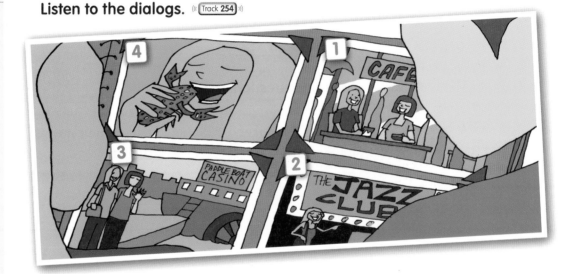

B
Listen Again

Listen again, and fill in the blanks. (((Track 255)))

1. She had _____ in the French Quarter.
2. She saw a band at a _____ club.
3. The boat on the river was really a _____.
4. She said the crayfish were _____.

C
Essential Expressions

Circle the correct word.

1. (Did / Do) you ever get lost when you were a child?
2. All in all, how (was / were) it?
3. By the end of the day, we were all (exhausted / exhausting).
4. Did I ever (tell / told) you about the time I cooked dinner for my parents?
5. I (hear / heard) this story about a family with a pet skunk.
6. It's a story about a boy who was (raised / raising) by apes.
7. Then what (happen / happened)?
8. Where was this picture (taken / took)?
9. Do you (remember / remembered) the first time you rode a bike?
10. I (have / had) a nice time during my visit to Ottawa.

Listening Practice

Listen. Write the answer. ((Track 256))

> He was nervous.   I fell into the water.   In Sydney.
>
> Two of my friends and I.   Two years ago.

1. _____
2. _____
3. _____
4. _____
5. _____

Listen. Write the question. ((Track 257))

> Can you tell us a joke?   Should I tell you how it ends?
>
> Were you hurt?   What did you do?   Where was it?

1. _____
2. _____
3. _____
4. _____
5. _____

Describe the picture using the words below.

listen	relax	tent	family

_____

_____

_____

_____

_____

✓ **Listen to the description of the picture.** ((Track 258))

Speaking Practice

A
Pronunciation Practice

In casual speech, you may hear the word "you" pronounced as "cha" or the words "your" or "you're" pronounced as "cher" after words that end with –t.

Written	Spoken
1. You've heard the joke before, haven't you?	1. You've heard the joke before, haven' cha?
2. Can't you remember the story?	2. Can' cha remember the story?
3. I told them what you're doing now.	3. I told them wha' cher doing now.

✓ **Now practice saying the following sentences.**

1. Then he said, "Drivers, start your engines!"
2. They want you to be in the picture with them.
3. Don't you want to watch a movie tonight?

✓ **Now listen and repeat.** (Track 259)

B
Conversation Pictures

Listen to the dialogs, and number the pictures. (Track 260)

✓ **Now listen to the dialogs again, and choose who likes the movie described.**

1. (A) Woman   (B) Man   (C) Both
2. (A) Woman   (B) Man   (C) Both
3. (A) Woman   (B) Man   (C) Both
4. (A) Woman   (B) Man   (C) Both

Short Dialogs

A

Dialog 1

Listen to the dialog and questions. Choose the best answer. ((Track 261))

1. (A) His cat   (B) Ice cream
   (C) Milk   (D) The keys

2. (A) It got a flat tire.   (B) Its engine had stopped.
   (C) It started moving.   (D) It was broken.

✓ **Listen again, and fill in the blanks.**

M: Did I ever tell you about the time I locked my keys in my car?

W: No. What happened?

M: I went to the store to buy some ❶_____.
I thought I'd only be in the store for a minute, so I didn't turn off the engine.

W: Uh oh. And then you ❷_____ the door when you got out of the car?

M: Yeah. I guess it is my ❸_____ whenever I get out of the car. So my car was running, but I was locked out of it! By the time the man showed up to open my car door, my car was ❹_____.

B

Dialog 2

Listen to the dialog and questions. Choose the best answer. ((Track 262))

1. (A) Answer the phone   (B) Clean the house
   (C) Cook for him   (D) Speak to him

2. (A) Find a new job   (B) Live with her mother
   (C) Not speak to her   (D) Pay twice as much

C

Dialog 3

Listen to the dialog, and complete each statement. ((Track 263))

1. The male speaker _____.

2. Pam _____.

Main Dialog

A

Listen

Listen to the dialog, and choose the best answer. (((Track 264)))

1. What are they talking about?
   - (A) A book she has read
   - (B) A class he took
   - (C) A movie he has seen
   - (D) A play they will watch

2. What is mysterious about Gatsby?
   - (A) His house
   - (B) His job
   - (C) His past life
   - (D) His wife

3. What was her opinion of the story?
   - (A) It was boring.
   - (B) It was pretty bad.
   - (C) It was terrible.
   - (D) It was good.

B

Listen Again

Listen again, and fill in the blanks. (((Track 265)))

W: What is that book you're carrying?

M: It's *The Great Gatsby* by Fitzgerald. I have to
   ❶_____ it for one of my classes.

W: Oh, I read that book **❷**_____.

M: Really? What is it about?

W: It's about a rich man with a mysterious
   ❸_____. He is in love with another **❹**_____
   man's wife. Of course, lots of **❺**_____ develop from this situation.

M: So it's a romance novel?

W: Not really. It's about the different **❻**_____ in society and how
   people can't really change who they are inside.

M: Is it any good? Do you think I'll **❼**_____ it?

W: I thought it was pretty **❽**_____.

Short Talks

Short Talk 1

Listen to the short talk and questions. Choose the best answer. ((Track 266))

1. (A) Her aunt   (B) Her mother
   (C) Her uncle   (D) The woman

2. (A) Boat   (B) Bus
   (C) Camel   (D) Taxi

✓ **Listen again, and fill in the blanks.**

I had a great time over the ❶＿＿＿＿＿＿
vacation. I went to Egypt with my aunt and uncle. My
❷＿＿＿＿＿＿ had always wanted to go there, and my
parents thought it would be a ❸＿＿＿＿＿＿ experience
for me. It was! We traveled by bus and taxi in the city, but
I also rode a ❹＿＿＿＿＿＿ in the desert. I'll never forget
seeing the Great Pyramid and the Sphinx.

B

Short Talk 2

Listen to the short talk and questions. Choose the best answer. ((Track 267))

1. (A) It was expensive.   (B) It was fun.
   (C) It went badly.   (D) It went well.

2. (A) After the movie   (B) Before eating
   (C) While talking   (D) Until Henry went home

C

Short Talk 3

Listen to the short talk, and fill in the chart. ((Track 268))

	Name:	Where:	Raised by:
1.	Romulus and Remus	_____	_____
2.	Mardevirin	_____	_____
3.	Pecos Bill	_____	_____

A

Picture Matching

Listen to the dialogs. Choose the correct picture. ((Track 269))

1. (A)　　　　(B)　　　　(C)

2. (A)　　　　(B)　　　　(C)

B

Listen & Choose

Listen to the dialogs and questions. Choose the best answer. ((Track 270))

3. (A) She is busy.　　　　(B) She is scared.
   (C) She found a ticket.　　(D) She might see it.

4. (A) Him　　　　　　　　(B) His friend
   (C) His friend's sister　　(D) His parents

5. (A) A kind wolf　　　　(B) A strong wind
   (C) Animals on a farm　(D) Pigs' houses

6. (A) At school　　　　(B) At the park
   (C) In a store　　　　(D) On the bus

7. (A) A dog　　　　　(B) An announcement
   (C) Candy　　　　　(D) Toys

8. (A) They liked the same girl.　(B) They lived together.
   (C) They were neighbors.　　(D) They were on the same baseball team.

9. (A) Movie posters　　(B) Paintings
   (C) Postcards　　　　(D) Nothing

A

Pre-listening Discussion

Talk about these questions.

1. Have you ever met a famous movie star?
2. If you saw a famous person on the street, would you say anything to her/him?
3. Have you been embarrassed in a store? What happened?

B

Listening Comprehension

Listen and answer the questions. ((Track 271))

1. **Who did the woman see in the ice cream store?**
   In the ice cream store, the woman saw _____.

2. **Why was he smiling at the woman?**
   He was smiling at her because _____.

3. **Where was her ice cream cone?**
   The ice cream cone was _____.

C

Dictation Practice

Listen again, and fill in the blanks. ((Track 272))

I heard this story from a ❶_____ of mine. He said it ❷_____ happened to a friend's mother's ❸_____.

One day, a lady ❹_____ into an ice cream store. She ❺_____ a strawberry ice cream cone for ❻_____. While she was waiting ❼_____ it, she noticed a man ❽_____ beside her. She looked ❾_____ and saw that he ❿_____ Harrison Ford! The lady had ⓫_____ all of his movies and ⓬_____ him, but she didn't ⓭_____ to act like some ⓮_____ fan in front of ⓯_____. Instead, she pretended to ⓰_____ cool, as if he was ⓱_____ another man in the ⓲_____ store.

When the lady ⓳_____ out of the store, she ⓴_____ she didn't have her ice cream ㉑_____. She went back ㉒_____ to get it and ㉓_____ Mr. Ford standing at the ㉔_____ and smiling. She smiled ㉕_____ and then told the ㉖_____ in the store, "I ㉗_____ my ice cream cone."

Mr. Ford ㉘_____, "No, you didn't. You ㉙_____ it in your ㉚_____ with your change."

Listening Test 🕐 08:53

PART I: Picture Description ((Track 273))

Listen and choose the statement that best describes what you see in the picture.

1.

(A)   (B)   (C)   (D)

2.

(A)   (B)   (C)   (D)

3.

(A)   (B)   (C)   (D)

4.

(A)　　　(B)　　　(C)　　　(D)

5.

(A)　　　(B)　　　(C)　　　(D)

PART II: Questions and Responses ((Track 274))

Listen and choose the best response to each question.

6. (A)　　　(B)　　　(C)

7. (A)　　　(B)　　　(C)

8. (A)　　　(B)　　　(C)

9. (A)　　　(B)　　　(C)

10. (A)　　　(B)　　　(C)

PART III: Short Conversations ((Track 275))

You will hear two dialogs, each followed by three questions. Listen carefully, and choose the best answer to each question.

11. What did the woman do on her vacation?

    (A) Saw some famous faces
    (B) Spent time in Paris
    (C) Took a photography class
    (D) Went on a cruise

12. What did the man want?

    (A) To visit Paris
    (B) To see the woman and her friend
    (C) To see some pictures of the woman's trip
    (D) To go to famous places around the world

13. Why did the woman enjoy her vacation?

    (A) She liked the photos she took.
    (B) She saw many famous places.
    (C) She danced a lot.
    (D) She spent a week abroad.

---

14. What is the main subject of the conversation?

    (A) The man's wish to travel more
    (B) The woman's experience at a hotel
    (C) Delicious breakfasts
    (D) Fancy beds

15. What did the woman not like about her hotel room?

    (A) The window was too large.
    (B) The room was too fancy.
    (C) The beds were too hard.
    (D) The rooms were too small.

16. What did the man say the woman needed?

    (A) Another vacation
    (B) A room with a better view
    (C) A good breakfast
    (D) To rest more

PART IV: Short Talks (((Track 276)))

You will hear two talks, each followed by three questions. Listen carefully, and choose the best answer to each question.

17. What was difficult for him during his vacation?
    (A) Paying high prices
    (B) The cold weather
    (C) Speaking the language
    (D) Walking everywhere

18. Which is true about the show he attended?
    (A) He didn't see it all.
    (B) He knew the story.
    (C) It was famous.
    (D) It was too long.

19. What did the speaker NOT say he did in London?
    (A) Saw three of the major museums in one day
    (B) Saw the Thames River
    (C) Went shopping
    (D) Listened to street musicians at Picadilly Circus

---

20. What kind of problem did the woman's husband have?
    (A) A cruel wife
    (B) A mental problem
    (C) A physical problem
    (D) A fear of animals

21. How did the doctor help him?
    (A) Gave him medicine
    (B) Operated on him
    (C) Talked to him
    (D) Talked to his wife

22. Why does the woman ask the doctor to change her husband back again?
    (A) So he can lay eggs
    (B) So he will like chickens
    (C) So he can fly
    (D) So he can speak to chickens